RICKY HATTON
The Real Hitman

The Official
Fly-on-the-Wall
Diary of a Champion

Dominic McGuinness

Main Photographer: Ben Duffy

GREAT NORTHERN

GREAT NORTHERN

Great Northern Books
PO Box 213, Ilkley, LS29 9WS
www.greatnorthernbooks.co.uk

First published 2006

ISBN: 1 905080 17 4

Design and layout: David Burrill

Photography: Ben Duffy
also Dominic Ingle, James McGoff, Mark Robinson, Paul Speak

Printed by Quebecor Ibérica, Barcelona

CIP Data
A catalogue for this book is available from the British Library

Acknowledgements

Thanks to all at the Phoenix Camp Gym and Team Hatton for their time and
assistance, in particular Paul Speak and the Hitman himself.

For Pat & Eil

CONTENTS

Foreword

by Stuart Pearce

I was aware of Ricky and his achievements in boxing long before I became manager of Manchester City in 2005 but it was only after I took the job I realised just how big a star he is in the North West.

Our paths crossed almost immediately as Ricky has a box at the football club and is a diehard blue. He's a very familiar figure around the place and everyone who works here has a good word for him.

After meeting him I was immediately impressed and could relate to him instantly. I invited him into our dressing room before a match and our friendship developed from there.

The thing that strikes me about him is that he's so level headed in what he wants to achieve. In both our professions it's easy to get carried away with people patting you on the back. With him, he's got a solid family base around him, probably similar to me in that respect. We have a friendship borne out of mutual respect.

In a society where one or two people will cut corners, you can tell when he's in that ring, that he's never cut a corner in his training regime. When I talk to young players in my profession, I tell them that if they take the odd shortcut on any one given day, it will reflect in their performance on match day.

Ricky's hard work in the gym from Monday to Friday, months in advance of bouts, makes all the difference when he's fighting. That's something I respect because some people can get by with a little bit of ability, take short cuts and then not achieve their full potential. Ricky's very single minded and he has a plan of where he wants to be in boxing. Along with that, he's an absolute pleasure to watch fight. He's an exciting, attacking fighter.

He's very level-headed, he's got his feet firmly on the ground, and no matter what he achieves you know what you're getting with him. He's not a bullshitter; you can tell that by just having a conversation with him. He gains respect everywhere because he's not full of crap. He speaks quite wisely and doesn't get carried away with his achievements. He knows the only achievement that counts is the next one.

Whatever you do in any sport you've got to be mentally tuned in and mentally strong. If you're not mentally strong when you get in that ring then you've got no hope. Many people have a good physique and a modicum of talent but I think the thing that gives you the edge as a footballer or a boxer is mental strength.

Quite often people aren't viewed until they've left the game. I think at the moment, I don't see a more exciting fighter anywhere. He can set Manchester alight on any one evening and I think he's not only a winner, it's the style in which he wins.

For me, he's put boxing back on the map.

Team Hatton

Billy Graham

AKA:	The Preacher
Occupation:	Trainer
Past life:	Professional Boxer
Division:	Middleweight
Record:	12 fights/10 wins (3 KOs)/2 defeats

Kerry Kayes

Occupation:	Nutrition/Strength Expert
	Managing Director, CNP Professional
Past lives:	'Mr Britain' Bodybuilder 1994
	British Karate Squad 1977
	Full Contact Fighter 1979
	Electrician

Ricky Hatton

AKA:	The Hitman
Occupation:	Professional Boxer
Past life:	Carpet Fitter
Division:	Light-welterweight/welterweight
Record:	41 fights/41 wins (30 KOs)/0 defeats
Height:	5'7"
Stance:	Orthodox
Date of birth:	06/10/78
Place of birth:	Stockport
Home town:	Hyde

Matthew Macklin
AKA: Matt
Occupation: Professional Boxer
Division: Light-middleweight
Record: 18/17 wins (13KOs)/1 defeat
Height: 5'10"
Stance: Orthodox
Date of birth: 14/5/82
Place of birth: Birmingham
Home town: Birmingham/Manchester

Matthew Hatton
AKA: Magic
Occupation: Professional Boxer
Division: Welterweight
Date of birth: 15/5/81
Record: 31 Fights/28 wins (11KOs)/
                  2 defeats/1 draw
Height: 5'8"
Stance: Orthodox
Place of birth: Stockport
Home town: Hyde

Ray Hatton
Punch Promotions
Occupation: Father/Manager
                  Carpet Fitting Business
Past life: Footballer - Manchester City FC
                  Publican
Home town: Hyde

Paul Speak
AKA: Speaky
Occupation: Friend/Agent/Dogsbody
                  (his description)
Past life: Greater Manchester Policeman
Home town: Radcliffe

Gareth Williams
Occupation: The Law Man
                  George Davies Solicitors
Home town: Bury

A Two Weight Champ

The small, dimly-lit, barely furnished dressing room is quiet. Ricky Hatton is sitting against a peeling white wall, beneath a pinned-up St George flag with the word 'England' emblazoned across the middle. The room's about the size of a boxing ring with toilets and a shower to the left of the entrance. It's no palace.

He's beaten the American champion, in his own backyard, to make history as the first Briton to win three successive world title fights.

Bandages are being carefully unravelled from his bruised hands as his mother sits beside him tenderly caressing the back of his head. The skin around his eyes is swollen and heavily marked. His head bowed as the last of the well-wishers is ushered out of the door.

There's no music, no wild celebration, just an air of relief, until Matthew Hatton breaks the atmosphere.... "it's all turned out nice again!" he pipes up in his best George Formby.

Ricky looks up and smiles as the Massachusetts doctor on duty gives him the once-over. "Everything seems fine," the medic reports, "but your nose is broken."

"You don't f****** say doc!" Ricky says with a smile. His nose has suffered more bad cracks than the audience at a Blackpool theatre during summer season.

A good half an hour after the unanimous decision handed the lad from Hyde the WBA welterweight title - his fourth title at two different weights - and he's still not out of his spangly, blue, tasselled, union flag encrusted shorts.

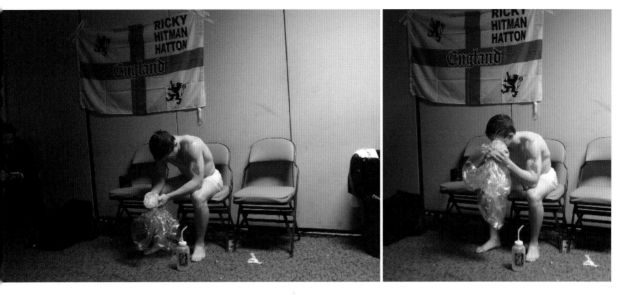

Post-fight, the room's vibe has changed significantly from the pre-bout banter played out to a soundtrack of Oasis and Stone Roses. Those that remain include the fighter, his parents Ray and Carole, his girlfriend Jennifer, brother Matthew, Mathew's girlfriend Gemma, trainer Billy Graham, his number two Kerry Kayes (also Ricky's fitness and nutrition guru), assistant and friend Paul Speak and cuts man Mick Williamson.

Eyes are trained on Ricky, who eventually looks up…. "I took some shots. It was like, bang! No need for that! I got déjà vu after a while. I was thinking, hang on, haven't you just hit me before!

"He was another f****** Eamonn Magee. I got him in the first round and thought, stay down ya ****!"

The wide grin and chuckle lift the mood. But it isn't as joyous an occasion as you might expect from a winner's dressing room. It seems everyone knows the fight with Collazo has raised questions about Ricky and his welterweight future.

"He was big!" Ray Hatton observes. "F****** well spotted!" Ricky spits back.

Laughter again fills the room before Ricky asks, "will someone get some ice for my left eye? I've got a right headache!"

It has been the hardest night of his professional career, but he has done it. He's beaten the American champion, in his own backyard, to make history as the first Briton to win three successive world title fights.

"It was like, bang! No need for that! I got déjà vu after a while. I was thinking, hang on, haven't you just hit me before!"

One Ricky Fatton

(Pic. Mark Robinson)

Rewind: Sunday, 5 June 2005......

2.35am......

The new IBF light-welterweight champion of the world rises off his knees as 20 thousand fight fans celebrate with a fervour you'd expect from a football crowd witnessing a last minute winner in the World Cup final. The shock of realising a dream and hammering the great Kostya Tszyu into an eleventh round submission still hasn't sunk in, but now he has one thought only.

"Get me that t-shirt," Ricky Hatton shouts to his corner as the usual well-wishers in the ring continue with the hugging, kissing and backslapping of their boy.

Trainer Billy Graham throws the black garment to the Hitman who manages to raise weary arms slowly and, with a little help, get the t-shirt over his sweaty and marked face.

Then, with the energy of a newborn spring lamb, he bounds up onto the ropes in front of the rows of assembled pressmen at ringside. He isn't looking for any of the British writers, he wants the Australians' full attention.

He sways on the ropes, like a kid on a playground climbing frame, and with the gloves that had pounded Tszyu's face and body still on his own bruised hands, he beats his chest and reveals the slogan printed in white on the black t-shirt – 'ONE RICKY FATTON' – it proclaims.

"Who's the f****** fatboy then?" Ricky bawls at them. "Not bad for a fat lad you Aussie bastards!"

He's made his point to those who had simply laughed when the 26 year-old 'kid' from a Manchester overspill estate had said, to the assembled journalists from down under at the Phoenix Camp Gym, that he would become the new 'man' at the MEN (Manchester Evening News) Arena.

Ricky knew what they'd been writing: he knew they considered him nothing but a chubby brawler who struggled to make the ten stone weight. He also knew, against all the odds, that he would beat the man that had ruled and struck fear into the division for a decade. And he did.

Ricky Hatton has made history. In the early hours of a June Sunday morning in Manchester, 2005, a packed house full of adoring fans roars him on to break the heart of the 35 year old proud legend. Thirty three minutes after the first bell, Tszyu is slumped on his stool when his trainer Johnny Lewis tells him he's pulling him out of the fight.

Referee Dave Parris makes the sweeping hand gesture to indicate the end of the fight and the place erupts. Everyone's caught up in the moment from Frank Bruno, Amir Khan and Gordon Ramsay at ringside, to vociferous locals in the nosebleed seats. Even Tszyu fans, like Hollywood star Russell Crowe, can only shake their heads and applaud.

There's a golden moment as the beaten warrior rises to acclaim the new king. When he can finally ease his battered body off his stool, Tszyu walks to the middle of the ring and raises Hatton's arm in a gesture of supreme sportsmanship that typifies everything that boxing should be.

"Kostya Tszyu was ranked number two pound-for-pound in any weight division," Ricky smiles at the retelling of the tale over a cup of coffee at the Betta Bodies gym in the Manchester suburb of Denton.

"One of the best light-welterweights of all time. All the way up to the fight nobody thought I could beat him. The only man that thought I could do it was me.

"It was unbelievable, and I'll tell you what, I've never known a man hit so hard in my life. Even the jabs, even in close, the little half-punches, they just hurt you. Especially the ones that hit me in the bollocks. He kept hitting me in the bollocks, but to be honest I got him with a better one didn't I!

(Pic. Mark Robinson)

"Every punch, he really hurt me. I was on my last legs myself. He quit after eleven rounds but I wasn't far behind him. I was dying. But I'll never forget the feeling when I looked over to the corner and saw the ref wave his hands. I was not only world champion, but undisputed world champion. Unbelievable."

Beating the Aussie-based Russian champion is, in his own words, 'a dream come true' for Ricky Hatton. It took a while to sink in, but after he left the bedlam of his over-excited post-fight dressing room that night, he had a couple of friends to become reacquainted with - Mr Guinness and Mr Dom Perignon.

His love of a night out is well documented. He's no enemy of fun. His post-fight party was always going to get messy.

"A little drink? That's an understatement to be honest," he says. "The fight was at two o'clock in the morning so by the time the fight had finished, it was three o'clock. Then I had a press conference so when I got away from the MEN Arena it was four o'clock.

"I went straight to the after-fight party at the Renaissance Hotel and I walked out of there at half-past-ten in the morning. The birds were tweeting. I was on such a high adrenalin-wise, and there were people still walking up and down the streets of Manchester singing, 'there's only one Ricky Hatton'. It was emotional stuff to be honest.

"It was more than just a boxing match, it was like an occasion and one I hope the fans in Manchester never forget.

"The next day I'd been offered, by several people, a big function: you know five-course meal and all that. I said no 'cos I'd already arranged to go to the local pub in Hattersley for a dodgy shirt day.

"I'm sure all the other champions do it – go to the local pub on their council estate and have a dodgy shirt day!"

By his own admission, Ricky revelled in the glory of the Tszyu fight for many weeks after that night in June. The video of those eleven rounds got more wear than even his favourite episode of *Only Fools and Horses*.

"For about two to three weeks after the fight I never had the tape off really. The first week, it was because I just had a real sense of achievement. It was such a massive buzz watching it. For the first week I was just filling up every time I watched it!"

Cat and Maussa

September 2005……

After a summer of basking in the glow of post-Kostya euphoria, it's back to business: with business being the operative word.

Team Hatton realised their true worth that night back at the MEN Arena in June and decide it's time for a change. That means leaving Frank Warren and his Sports Network, although the promoter isn't too happy about this and alleges breach of contract.

Warren claims he struck a four-fight deal with Ricky before the Kostya Tszyu showdown. He wants to promote those three remaining fights, and is not going to step aside quietly. According to Team Hatton, they had a fight-by-fight agreement so are free to move on. In their eyes, it's a case of whoever can deliver the fights they want, with the biggest purse, gets the gig and jobs a good 'un.

Step forward Robert Waterman and Dennis Hobson of Sheffield-based Fight Academy.

Rather than take an easy option, a deal's struck for a unification bout with the WBA light-welterweight champion Carlos Maussa of Columbia. As Frank Warren has secured the exclusive rights to the Hitman's spiritual home, the MEN Arena, Ricky and his supporters will have to cross the Pennines for the fight at Sheffield's Hallam FM venue on Saturday 26 November.

The 34-year-old Maussa is a tricky opponent who knocked out Vivian Harris in his previous fight and has mixed it with the likes of Miguel Angel Cotto.

There is, however, a threat to the fight taking place after Warren seeks an injunction preventing Ricky from fighting for any other promoter. The injunction is dropped after the Hatton camp serve witness statements.

But still Ricky's preparations are hardly going smoothly.

There's another twist when it's revealed that Warren has signed WBA mandatory challenger Souleymane M'baye. The Frenchman makes a late legal bid to force a postponement or cancellation of Hatton v Maussa. Lawyers for M'baye argue in a New York courtroom that Maussa should not defend the WBA belt against anyone but him, but the plea is rejected.

Saturday, 26 November 2005……

So the fight is given the green light, but there is still time for another trauma. With just a few hours of valuable relaxing time to go before Ricky is due at the arena, the hotel he's staying at is evacuated due to a gas leak. Ricky is forced to spend an hour in a friend's car trying to keep warm until the problem is fixed.

Eventually it's down to business at the Hallam FM Arena. As ever at a Hatton fight, the atmosphere is boisterous inside the venue with, as expected, thousands of Hatton fans in attendance despite the switch to Yorkshire. Among them, Manchester City boss Stuart (Psycho) Pearce who leads the Hatton procession to the ring with Ricky's IBF belt held aloft as the strains of *Blue Moon* are belted out over the PA.

"I think we had a game that day and then I went over," Psycho later said. "I live in Wiltshire so it was a bummer of an evening driving over to Sheffield then back down to Wiltshire on my own. But it was one of those fights when you know you've got to get over there and show a bit of support.

"I popped in to see him before the fight. I went into the dressing room and he said 'would you like to take one of the belts into the ring?' I told him that I'd really prefer not to 'cos I was just there to watch the fight. I didn't want to be centre stage.

"But I was talked into it; I was told it'd be a really proud moment for Ricky if I did it. So when I found out it'd mean a great deal to him, I did it."

Ricky knows it's going to be a tough night when, within the first 30 seconds of the first bell, a clash of heads results in a bad cut around his left eye. Blood is dripping from his right eye a round later.

But trusty cuts man (and London cabbie) Mick Williamson stems the flow of blood to give the Hitman a clear sight of the lanky Colombian. He battles through that early nightmare and unleashes a sensational left-hook in the ninth round, which dumps Maussa to the canvas for the first time in his career. He's counted out after one minute and ten seconds of the round.

With one of the best punches of his career, Ricky Hatton has unified the IBF and WBA light-welterweight titles.

Naseem Hamed is among those watching at ringside as Ricky takes the microphone and, live on Sky Sports, dedicates the victory to his father Ray.

"This [WBA belt] is the third world title I've won... and I'd like to dedicate this belt to my dad and give it to my dad.

"This is the hardest period of my boxing career, and what my dad has done for me in the build-up in the last few months, he deserves this belt more than I do."

December 2005......

Ricky's giving his thoughts on the Maussa fight a few weeks after his victory. He's not in a serious mood.

"He was awkward," he begins, "about six foot tall and ugly. Big ears! He looked like a Ford Fiesta with both the doors open!

"Within three rounds I had a cut over my left eye, a cut over my right eye. He had a better head on him than Denis Law. He nutted me left, right and centre.

"He was so tall he kept pulling away from my punches and I was swinging and swinging trying to catch him. I was missing by two inches every time so I went back to the corner and I said, 'Billy, he's too tall. He's leaning back. What do you think I should do?' He said, 'just keep swinging, hopefully the draft will give him pneumonia!'

"But this one punch, I just caught him and cracked him right on the chin. It was just one of those punches where you take a run-up, launch it, and knock him out. To be honest, if he'd got up, I'd have f****** jumped out!"

(Pic. Mark Robinson)

Who's Next?

Thursday, February 9, 2006........

In the wake of the victory over Carlos Maussa, inevitably attention has switched to Ricky's next opponent. A fight with Floyd Mayweather Jnr is the Holy Grail, but he's now stepped up to welterweight, and in any case that fight won't be made just yet.

In the interim, the options aren't too clear. Will Ricky stay at 140lbs or step up a division, like Gatti and Mayweather have done?

It is again down to Dennis Hobson and Robert Waterman of Fight Academy to come up with the goods. Team Hatton has opted to stay loyal to the two promoters after they delivered on a promise to set up the Maussa fight, and, in doing so, enabled Ricky to claim another belt.

A press conference has been called, despite no opponent being confirmed, for the news that Ricky Hatton is to go Stateside - the 'American Invasion'.

The media has gathered on the HMS Belfast on the River Thames. It has been revealed that Ricky has signed a three-fight deal with Fight Academy and, Philadelphia-based, Banner Promotions.

Carlos Baldomir, who shocked the boxing world by beating Zab Judah in January 2006, appears to be the front runner opponent for Ricky's top-of-the-bill American debut. Other names in the mix include Arturo Gatti and Acelino Frietas. All will become much clearer once the bidding war for Ricky's signature, between HBO and Showtime, is settled.

Wednesday, 15 February......

There's another fight on Ricky's mind this week as he flies to New York to face a court action brought by French boxer Souleyman M'baye.

He is suing Hatton for $3m loss of earnings after the Hitman chose to face Carlos Maussa rather than face M'baye, who claims he should have faced the Colombian for the WBA light-welterweight title rather than Hatton.

With training for the May 13 fight about to start, this is an unwelcome distraction. Ricky will be Stateside for five days while he and his solicitor Gareth Williams give depositions.

Promoter Dennis Hobson, Fight Academy.

With M'baye now managed by Frank Warren, the court action has added a new twist to events taking place outside the ring.

Monday, 20 February......

If the journey Stateside was a headache for Ricky, it proved to be an even bigger one for Gareth Williams. One evening the pair were walking in Times Square when somebody recognised Ricky and approached him to say hello. While Ricky turned to chat to the fan, Gareth was punched to the ground in a random, unprovoked attack. He didn't see it coming, didn't get a proper look at the attacker, who sprinted away, and was left with a nasty cut above his left eye and concussion.

"There are a lot of strange people in New York," Ricky said on their return. "I was shaking someone's hand, I turned round and someone had attacked Gareth. You wouldn't believe it. Funny!"

No doubt Gareth's sides were as split as his head.

Wednesday, 22 February......

The mood in the camp has been lifted with the news that Ricky's been dropped from the lawsuit between Souleymane M'baye and the WBA, leaving him clear to stage his next fight in America. M'baye, the WBA mandatory contender, had asked a federal court in New York to bar Hatton, the WBA light-welterweight champion, from taking a fight against anyone other than M'baye for his next bout.

Ricky's attorney Scott Shaffer argued that an

American court was not the proper place for a dispute between M'baye, a Frenchman, and Hatton, an Englishman. M'baye's attorney Judd Burstein withdrew the complaint.

The case continues, between M'baye and the WBA, on M'baye's claim that he's been denied a title shot.

Monday, 13 March......

A plaque has been unveiled at Ricky's old home, the New Inn Pub in Hattersley. Ricky is a proud man today.

"The Hattersley estate is where I was born and my mum and dad had the pub for nine years. The plaque on the wall says, 'Ricky Hatton – light-welterweight champion – was born and lived in Hattersley. In recognition of his achievements, the people's champion'.

"You hear of people having plaques and streets named after them, so stuff like this never ceases to amaze me. It's brilliant."

Tuesday, 14 March......

Although it has taken a little longer than usual, a deal has now been done by Fight Academy for Ricky to fight former lightweight contender, Juan Lazcano, on Saturday 13 May.

Wednesday, 15 March......

Just as promoter Dennis Hobson is preparing to announce the details, there is bad news from the US: the Texan has broken a finger in training.

Meanwhile, Carlos Baldomir, the WBC welterweight champion and Hatton's preferred choice, has signed to fight Arturo Gatti, another long-term prospective Hitman opponent.

"It has been a tiny bit frustrating," Hobson says. "First we had to step away from the negotiating table while Ricky's court case in the US was going on and then, just as we signed what we thought would be the perfect opponent for Ricky to make an American statement with, he pulls out hurt. But these things happen, it is no big deal."

What Fight Academy does consider a big deal, however, is the lucrative one they've struck with TV Stateside.

"We've agreed a fantastic three-fight deal for Ricky with HBO," Hobson says. "It will ensure that not only will Ricky receive much more money per fight than he did before he signed with us, but also that more American fans will get to see Ricky on US TV than ever before."

Thursday, 16 March......

Ricky takes advantage of a chance to meet one of his heroes as heavyweight legend Mike Tyson is in Manchester. While talks concerning his next opponent continue, the Hitman has dinner with Iron Mike.

"Tyson won the heavyweight title as a twenty year old!" Ricky says with eyes wide in amazement. "What an absolute monster! Imagine finding him in bed with your missus? You'd f****** tuck him in wouldn't you!"

Friday, 17 March......

Although WBA business has been settled for the time being, the IBF has ordered Ricky to make a mandatory defence against Australian-based Tunisian, Naoufel Ben Rabah. That isn't a match HBO is particularly interested in. Team Hatton has 30 days to make a move.

(Pic. Paul Speak)

"Tyson won the heavyweight title as a twenty year old! What an absolute monster! Imagine finding him in bed with your missus - you'd f**** tuck him in wouldn't you!"**

The Showman

One day in the monastery is pretty much like any other. In a bid to combat the boredom of the boxer's often solitary existence when training, Ricky is keen to keep his evening social diary as busy as possible.

With the pub now out of bounds, and no repeats of 'Only Fools and Horses' on the telly, there are thankfully still plenty of opportunities at this stage of fight preparation for Ricky to get out and meet the people.

Not surprisingly, given his demeanour and accessibility, invites to events all over the country are constantly dropping through the door. Inevitably, many are dismissed for geographical reasons, but sometimes the lure of a good Sportsman's Dinner – and a bit of extra pocket money – will grab the Hitman. Not that cash is the driving force for making such an appearance. Boxers are showmen after all and the chance to exhibit one's talent, in whatever form, can be an intoxicating thing.

And when it comes to after-dinner speaking for a laddish, beer-sodden crowd, Ricky can hold his own with the best of them. He's obviously picked up some tips from his mate, and fellow Blue, Bernard Manning, in how to hold a crowd. Particularly a boisterous one.

This evening, Ricky's hosting a question and answer session at a Sportsman's Dinner at the Queen's Hotel in Leeds. An interesting prospect as Yorkshire folk aren't always the most welcoming to those from the other side of the Pennines.

Also, as a result of agreeing to appear at the 'do', Ricky will miss Manchester City's fourth-round rearranged FA Cup tie at home to West Ham. The boy's a trouper!

The Hitman's in verbal rather than physical action in front of what might be a tough crowd. This is his rival Junior Witter's neck of the woods, and, you never know, maybe a few lagered-up lads will throw a few heckles his way.

8.30pm……

The Queen's Hotel is slap bang in the city centre and it's soon obvious that this is the right place. Burly blokes, bursting out of monkey suits, are milling around the bar outside the function room. As is the case these days, it's not a men-only affair and there's a sprinkling of glammed-up ladies tottering about precariously in high heels, many looking more gangsters-moll than sporting-enthusiast.

In the main room there are 300 or so punters seated, tucking into a roast with all the trimmings. In the middle of the room is a boxing ring. Those gathered are looking forward to three bouts involving local fighters, as well as hearing from the guest of honour, whilst stuffing themselves with booze and a hearty feed.

The top table is to the left of the entrance of the square room. Sitting up there, alongside the main attraction, is Brendan Ingle, who's made the short journey up from Sheffield. Other names dotted about the room include British and Commonwealth cruiserweight, Mark Hobson, who recently fought, and narrowly lost a WBU clash with Enzo Maccarinelli.

There's a lull between the main course and dessert. Ricky looks bored as he tinkers with his mobile phone, and pulls at his royal blue dickie bow. Did he consider pulling out of tonight's function in order to watch City?

"Well I should have been there, but obviously this dinner was booked weeks in advance and I didn't know the game would be rearranged," he explains in his broad Mancunian accent. "Also, you know, this is nearly as much a part of my job as fighting.

"My mum doesn't know what boxing's all about. She thought sugar diabetes was a Welsh flyweight!"

Maybe not as much, but it's still part of my job and people have paid good money to come and watch me so you can't let them down.

"I'm just happy to be here and I was never going to pull out. Each time you come to these events you meet new fans. Hopefully, people will say 'wasn't Ricky Hatton good, wasn't he a nice fella, let's go and watch him fight'. It is part of your job and it broadens your horizons."

Because of the nature of this particular speaking engagement, Ricky will find himself performing from inside the very familiar environment of a boxing ring, albeit in a very different situation. A tuxedo, black shirt and bright bowtie replacing the more customary spangly blue shorts. Another dangerous weapon, the microphone, will be held in a lethal left hand more used to the feel of a boxing glove and his opponents' ribs.

He'll be in a ring, but how comfortable will he be with all eyes on him; people hanging off his every word, hoping for a withering one-liner rather than a crippling body shot?

"This is the easy part," he says as a grin breaks across his face. "I know when I get in that ring I'm not gonna get hit!

"There are actually three fights on tonight so I'm not doing my full stand-up. Normally I get up there and talk for 45 minutes but with three fights to get through I'm just going to do a question and answer session for 15 or 20 minutes because they want to get the boxing started. An easy night all round. Hopefully I'll get some good questions and go down well."

The room is full, every table filled. Not a bad feat considering the fact that this event falls on the very same evening the legend that is Mike Tyson is guest speaker at a function about a mile away at Elland Road, home of Leeds United AFC.

"It's a strange one really," Ricky ponders as he waves away dessert. "You'd have thought the people that organised it would have realised that me and Tyson were speaking on the same night and maybe altered it. But you know I find it very pleasing and an honour that I've still sold out. There are some former champions here and some big names so it shows you how highly they think of me and I'm very happy."

Plates are clanking and clattering as flustered waiters and waitresses hustle to clear the tables as Ricky leaves his seat and makes his way to the middle of the ring.

The main lights are dimmed, there's a hush around the room and then a few of the over-excited encourage others to shut up by almost shouting 'ssshhhhhhhhhhhh'. It's a bit like a minute's silence at a football ground when the well-intentioned supporters make more noise, during the supposed period of quiet, than the confused drunks and hecklers.

Ricky breaks into a beaming smile as he leans against the ropes, mic in hand. He looks oddly small in there in his civvies while the master of ceremonies reminds the audience they're in the presence of greatness, "The IBF and WBA light-welterweight champion of the world.........RIIIICCCCKKKYY HATTON!"

Not quite Jimmy Lennon Junior, but not a bad effort and it inspires uproarious applause as Ricky starts to work the crowd, moving about the ring as his act begins.

"When I speak at these events," he says, "I tend to swear a lot, so apologies to the ladies if I use those four-letter words they so dislike, you know like COOK, WASH and IRON!" The assembled hoot, whistle and cheer.

"Anyway, thanks for the invite. It's great to see some of the fighters here, and the likes of Brendan Ingle on the top table. There are some old f*****s on that top table; it's like a Chapel of Rest!" Ricky's up and running.

"Before we start, how are City getting on? What? One-down? Oh f****** hell!"

The entertainer then invites questions. The hands go up, and his friend and assistant, Paul Speak, heads out with a microphone to make them heard. The first question gets the ball rolling – a nice easy one to start as a middle-aged chap asks him how he got into boxing.

"Well normally it's passed down from your father or grandfather, but no-one in my family had ever done boxing. We're mainly a football family. In fact my father was very, very fortunate to have played for the greatest football team the world's ever seen, Manchester City!"

There are more cheers than boos at this news. Hardly surprising as a Leeds crowd would join forces with the Devil himself if they thought he might share their hatred of Manchester United. Ricky, of course, knows this.

"If there's one thing I can't stand, it's Manchester United!" Cue loud cheers all round. "And if there's one thing I can't stand more than Manchester United, it's Ruud Van Nistelrooy. What a waste of space that man is. He's on his arse more than his feet!

"The other day there was nothing on the telly and United were playing. I thought, 'I'm not watching this shit', so I decided to do some hoovering.

"I hoovered around the coffee table, then around the settee, around the fireplace, around the armchairs and around the television. As I hoovered around the TV, I bumped it and Van Nistelrooy fell over in the box!

"He fell that fast he's fighting Audley Harrison next!"

Ricky pauses to soak in the applause like a seasoned pro. This is, afterall, a man who has Roy 'Chubby' Brown's suit framed in his living room. He's obviously picked up plenty of tips.

"But if my dad was here," the Hitman continues, "you'd just take one look at him and wonder how had he produced a world champion fighter? He's no bigger than yer man over there." Ricky points at a little bald old bloke sitting near the ring. This prompts more hilarity and some uncomfortable shifting from the butt of the joke.

"But my mother on the other hand, and God knows I love her, but I think the best way to describe my mum is simply ... monster!'"

He's got them in the palm of his hand now.

"Her rice crispies don't go 'snap, crackle and pop' in the morning, they go 'f*** me she's coming!'

"My mum, she does support me the best she can but she doesn't know what boxing's all about. She thought sugar diabetes was a Welsh flyweight!

"But no-one in the family had ever done it. I did kick-boxing. I was into all the Bruce Lee films so I thought 'I'll do kick-boxing'. Because I'd always been the short, stocky type I was always giving five or six inches reach to my opponent. I was always good with my fists but never with my feet, so I'd basically always try and get close to my opponent. But when you're giving away five or six inches in height and reach, to put it bluntly, I was getting my f****** head kicked in.

Q: Will you win your next fight Ricky?   A: Does a bear shit in the woods?

But when you're giving away five or six inches in height and reach, to put it bluntly, I was getting my f****** head kicked in.

"So I said to my kick-boxing coach that my talent was with my fists not my feet and I was going to take up boxing. I walked over to the local boxing gym in Hyde, my hometown.

"So the boxing started from there. Normally it's passed on through the generations but it was never the case with us, so it's a bit of a puzzle."

Questions come thick and fast, all handled expertly by the man in the middle of the ring, one hand in pocket, leaning back when he talks. He looks like he's stepped off the set of the 70s TV show *The Comedians*. All that's missing is the odd mother-in-law gag as Ricky pads out his anecdotes with all manner of jokes.

The microphone's handed to a tall, skinny man in his thirties with shoulder length blonde hair. Before he can ask his question, Ricky fixes him with a steely stare, turns to another part of the audience for effect, and lets rip.

"He looks like Robbie Savage," he says pointing at the poor bloke who doesn't know where to look. "I'd love to punch f*** out of him." The crowd erupts, all eyes on the not-so-savage look-a-like.

The accused stands his ground though, takes the abuse on the chin with good humour, and gets in his question, asking whether or not Ricky ever expected to get so famous.

"Not really," he says, "but fame's never been high on my list of priorities. If I could earn the money, win the titles and have the success without the fame, I'd be happy with that. You never think a lad from the streets of Manchester would get to this stage. You never do.

"I was born in Hattersley, a council estate which is very rough. It was better known for the Moors murderers, and obviously with Harold Shipman and what he did in Hyde, it's nice to do a little bit of good for the area. Coming from a council estate, I'd like to think that kids, whatever they do – football or boxing – can say 'well if Ricky can do it then so can I'. I think that's what sport in general is all about."

Ricky signs off by telling the assembled it's been a pleasure talking to them. The response is loud continued applause, whistles and shouts of 'go on Ricky' and a standing ovation all around the room. He's gone down well in Leeds.

"Fame's never been high on my list of priorities. If I could earn the money, win the titles and have the success without the fame, I'd be happy with that."

Luis Collazo, WBA welterweight champion.

Tuesday, 21 March......

Fight Academy reaches a deal with promoter Don King for Ricky to move up to welterweight to challenge Luis Collazo for his WBA title.

So after injuries, speculation and debate, it's finally confirmed that the Hitman will be fighting Collazo, a New Yorker of Puerto Rican origin who has a decent, yet unheralded, record of 27-1.

Originally the fight had been scheduled to take place at the Foxwoods Casino in Connecticut, but along with the change of weight and fighter, Ricky is happy with a venue switch.

"It's going to be in Boston now because of the sales of tickets," he says. "Connecticut isn't as big, so we want it in Boston now, which is 45 minutes down the road, and the venue there holds 17 thousand.

"He's the WBA welterweight champion and I'm moving up a weight to try and become a two-weight world champion.

"The terms have been agreed; everything's done. Don King is his promoter and they've given it the thumbs up. It's been difficult with HBO not accepting certain fighters, but it's now sorted."

> **"He's the WBA welterweight champion and I'm moving up a weight to try and become a two-weight world champion."**

Phoenix Camp Gym

Wednesday, 22 March......

Midday......

The stairs in the old hat factory building are rickety and winding. There's been no love laboured over the interior design. The walls are bare except for the odd poster advertising a forthcoming karate contest.

At the top of the stairs, more stairs, then a door leading into the Betta Bodies Gym.

The long room is awash with equipment. At first glance it's almost like a factory, but the workers tending these machines are not ordinary looking. All manner of free-weights are here along with the odd bike, rowing machine, treadmill and stepper thrown in for good measure.

The roof above looks a little tatty. Haphazard skylights provide the daylight in curious sunny shafts throughout the room.

To the left of the entrance is a little canteen. There's a man at least five foot wide, wearing a black, sleeveless t-shirt tucking into what looks like a boring feed of pasta. He's probably in his late forties with veins bulging out of his massive arms, neck and head.

The narrow gym is cluttered. There's barely room to manoeuvre between the static steel machines and those of the human kind. This is a serious bodybuilding place.

At the end of the room, 40 yards or so, it's a right turn to the double doors where the sign confirms it's Billy Graham's gym. According to a large round sticker on the door, it has Dorian Yates's approval. From the sticker and the face in the middle of it, it would appear Yates is/was a bodybuilder of renown who has a nice line in foodstuffs that can help make your muscles rather big.

Through the double doors and the first thing that hits you is the stifling humid heat. The second is the smell – an odd musty mix of sweat and leather. There's a full-size boxing ring straight in front of the doors, and beyond that bags of various weights hang from the ceiling either side of a long steel bar. This is 'the bar' that boxers jump over as part of their training regime.

At the end of the gym lies something that looks like an office with a huge glass cabinet at one end. On closer inspection it's apparent that this 'cabinet' is the home of a large iguana.

Billy 'the Preacher' Graham owns the lizard, or Liston as he's known after the boxer of the same name. The beast is perched on a log in the tank. It doesn't move. It looks stuffed.

Running parallel to Liston's office is a changing room with a dark corridor separating the two. It's basic with a couple of benches and a shower at the end.

"I beat the best man at light-welterweight (Kostya Tszyu) and I'm now going for a new title. I'm not saying I'm going to stay at welterweight but you've got to keep setting new goals for yourself."

Three large windows down the right hand side of the main room let in light and offer limited views of Denton's backstreets, while all around the other three walls are framed posters advertising fight nights gone by, or framed photos of fighters with other fighters, or fighters pictured with celebrities.

The largest of the lot shows a smiling Ricky Hatton, sunbathing on a deckchair, wearing just a pair of large, white y-fronts pulled up to his chest. Next to him is Manchester comedian, Bernard Manning, also grinning, and dressed the same. Somehow you get the feeling Bernard hasn't adjusted his underwear for effect.

This picture was taken shortly before Ricky went into training for the Kostya Tszyu fight. He weighed 13 stone at the time. How can he put on, then lose, 42 pounds in a matter of weeks?

The room is empty until, suddenly, there's a burst of sound from inside the changing room, a door's flung open and out jogs Ricky 'the Hitman' Hatton dressed from head-to-toe in a black sweat suit and black trainers.

He nods, fires off a quick "y'right mate" before jogging over to a heavy bag and landing what

would be a left-hook body shot fit to floor a contrary elephant.

As Ricky continues to work on the bag as if it had called his mum a slag, in walks the man who shares the name of the gym.

Billy Graham strides into his office, drops his gym bag and starts stripping off layers of clothes without saying a word.

He's ready for work now, dressed in a sleeveless white t-shirt (also advertising Dorian Yates and his products) revealing heavily tattooed, muscle-bound arms, grey tracksuit bottoms and

white boxing boots.

The tattoos are a mixture. There's Muhammad Ali's face on one arm, and various creatures – frogs, lizards and odd things – on the other. Billy likes reptiles, amphibians and snakes. He keeps them as pets at home in Mossley.

Now 50, he has a weathered face that looks like it's seen more than a little of the edgier side of life. His bulging eyes and gruff, heavy Salford accent, give him a fearsome air at times.

1.00pm......

For each training camp, Ricky eases himself back into the groove. Unlike many fighters who are happy to train for eight weeks leading up to a fight, the Hitman insists on a three-month training programme.

The extra weeks are essential for a man who, by his own admission, when off-training, likes to get stuck-in to curries and Chinese food, all washed down with plenty of Guinness. He is, in his own words, a 'takeaway merchant' and his love of a pint is legendary.

But when a fight is approaching, and a date has been set, he has another, even more important, date of his own to keep. He heads off into the kitchen and picks the relevant day and makes a neat circle around that date on the calendar. The fugitive is back in his monastery.

It's been four weeks since Ricky set his date. His diet has improved, he's cut out the rubbish and started to up his intake of the required nutrients.

Training to this point has been light, and dull, consisting of work on the bags, pads and weights, followed by a run in the evening.

Now, with Luis Collazo fixed for May 13 and eight weeks to go, the work gets serious. A boxing training camp is not what most people would call fun.

"I most enjoy the body-belt," Ricky shouts above the tedious chatter of some local radio DJ, blaring out from the gym's ghetto blaster. "Obviously you need your sparring, that is where you get your timing, and you have to get your sparring partners in the mirror image of your opponent, that's a vital part of your training.

"But I do love the body-belt, 15 rounds on the body-belt. The pace that I go at is absolutely ferocious, and the minute I've done that I know, from a stamina point of view and a conditioning point of view, that I don't need to worry. That's probably the best part of my training.

"I think the worst part of my training is the running because it's basically boring really. You find yourself going on different runs to make it a bit more exciting but it never tends to work, you're bored to tears.

"For the fight against Kostya Tszyu, I was running at two in the morning, and there's nothing out there. I mean there are no cars, no traffic, bats flying out of the trees and things rustling in the bushes. It can be scary. Yeah, the roadwork is definitely the worst part.

"The dieting isn't much fun either because I love my food. I think that's pretty clear to see at times," he adds with a chuckle.

Whilst other British fighters, including Lennox Lewis, Frank Bruno and Nigel Benn, enjoyed setting up training camps on foreign shores, it isn't something Team Hatton has ever done.

The benefits of training at altitude have long been argued, but the Hitman won't swap the polluted environs of Denton and Hyde for the apparent wholesome crisp air of the mountains.

"A lot of people go to Tenerife or Big Bear, a resort 100 miles north-east of Los Angeles, to train with all the altitude and that. Some people go there just to convince themselves in their own mind.

"I don't mean to blow my own trumpet, but you show me another fighter that's fitter or throws as many punches as me!

"Going to Tenerife or wherever, it sounds the part, but I don't think it's all that."

Ricky continues to pound the bag as a couple of random local youths wander in to watch the action. This is one fighter who doesn't believe in locking himself away, denying himself the company of family and friends in a bid to stay focused.

Thursday, 23 March......

The Hitman can sell 20 thousand tickets for any fight on any given night in Manchester. Fighting an American in Boston is a gamble.

Living in the shadow of its bigger neighbour New York, the city hasn't staged a major fight since 'Marvellous' Marvin Hagler knocked out Vito Antuofermo at the old Boston Garden 25 years ago.

The US boxing public is not easily won over when it comes to British fighters and Hatton v Collazo is to be staged at a 17 thousand-seater venue.

"For a British fighter to go over to the United States and sell that many tickets, well there's no other fighter in England could do that," Ricky says. "That's a huge thing in my favour.

"I'm the biggest ticket seller in England by far, and I'd like to think there'll be thousands of fans over to watch me. That'll go down well with the American press."

A sell-out Stateside would also go some way in settling the argument over who's the biggest name in British boxing today – Hatton or super-middleweight Joe Calzaghe.

Calzaghe's dismantling of the feared Jeff Lacy has been heralded by some in the game as the

finest performance by a Brit – ever.

"Well me and Joe have similar records," Ricky says. "He's 41 and 0 and I'm 40 and 0, and with Joe's brilliant recent win you'll always get people saying, 'I think Joe's number one pound-for-pound, or I think Ricky's number one pound-for pound'. People can make their own decisions about that, but I think it's clear, without a shadow of a doubt; I'm the biggest ticket seller in England.

"I think in Kostya Tszyu, I beat someone who was the world's number two pound-for-pound in any boxing division. One of the best light-welterweights ever.

"Jeff Lacy isn't one of the best super-middleweights of all time and he certainly wasn't in the top ten pound-for-pound fighters. I don't want to take anything away from Joe's performance, but it should be put in perspective.

"It's not Joe that's saying all this. Me and Joe are mates and we get on like a house on fire.

"People will always come to their own conclusions, but Kostya Tszyu beat umpteen world champions in his time, Jeff Lacy had only had 22 fights. That's my view on it."

The subject of the legal actions hanging over Team Hatton is raised.

"Well there's no situation really," Ricky says, shrugging his shoulders. "When Frank Warren offered me a contract and I didn't agree to it, I left it for a better deal to better myself and he wasn't too happy.

"He claimed he had a contract and that was about nine months ago. He then tried to get an injunction to stop me fighting Carlos Maussa.

"He also signed a number one contender, Souleymane M'baye, who then commenced legal proceedings against me.

"Every way he's tried to get to me, he's failed. The situation now with Frank Warren is that I've been advised not to worry about litigation, but my dad's been dragged into it. He's even gone a stage further by suing me dad for defamation.

Ricky's normally bright demeanour is now somewhat darker.

"He's suing my dad for libel over comments he said in a radio interview. But my dad's defending the case. He doesn't think he's done anything wrong. That's that really.

"Every time Frank's put something towards us we've beaten him. Now he's going for my dad. He's defending himself just like I am.

"Frank can write what he wants in articles or whatever, but since I've left him, I've got a world title, am going for another and I'm topping the bill in America, which is something I've wanted to do for God knows how long. Dennis Hobson and his Fight

Academy got me the Carlos Maussa fight, which was very good of them. They've got me this fight, where I'm stepping up a weight, so the dreams that I've waited for are coming true.

"People ask if I feel like I made a mistake in leaving Frank. Are these people stupid? Earning more money, topping the bill in America, moving up a weight and challenging for these titles!

"It is costing me a bit of expense in going to court to put my case forward with Frank, but to be honest, even with the money I put forward for court costs, I'm still quids in."

The split from Warren has come at another cost though. At present, Ricky is unable to fight at his spiritual home - the MEN Arena.

"Yeah, unfortunately I can't fight there anymore," Ricky says with the shake of his head. "Frank Warren has exclusive rights there, but the fans know. My message to the fans is: I'd love to fight in Manchester, but the reason I can't fight in Manchester is through no fault of Ricky Hatton."

Friday, 24 March……

12.35pm……

The black BMW X5 pulls up outside the large red-brick building, which lies next to the busy M67 on the edge of Denton.

Ricky Hatton's pretty much on time. He makes his way up the stairs and through the Betta Bodies Gym to the Phoenix Camp Gym at the back of the room with his kit bag slung over his shoulder. As ever, a baseball cap is pulled down tightly over his eyes. Not that this does anything to stop anyone in the gym knowing exactly who the little fella in the navy tracksuit bottoms and training coat is. That said, apart from the odd wink or nod from the lads working out, all veins and muscles bulging as they lift, nobody bothers him.

After slipping into his all-black sweat suit, Ricky walks over to Billy Graham, who's busy strapping his large bony hands, makes an inaudible gag at his trainer's expense, laughs, clambers through the ropes of the ring and starts to shadow box in front of the huge mirror on the left-hand wall.

"I'm starting to up it now as the days go by," he shouts between grunts. "I'm moving up a weight to fight for a welterweight title so I've got the opportunity to become a double world champion.

It's a massive, massive fight for me. If winning a world title at one weight wasn't enough, to become a double weight world champion is something very special."

Ricky's on a roll now as he flicks out jabs, hooks and uppercuts on his imaginary opponent.

"I beat the best man at light-welterweight [Kostya Tszyu] and I'm now going for a new title. I'm not saying I'm going to stay at welterweight but you've got to keep setting new goals for yourself.

"When I beat Kostya Tszyu, in many ways that was my Mount Everest and I've had a lot of fights. I don't really want to be going much more than three years, so I want the defining fights, the big-meaning fights where hopefully it'll cement my legacy. In 20 years people might still be talking about me. So that's the craic."

At this point, Matthew Macklin, Irish middleweight champion but a natural light-middleweight, closes the changing room door behind him and passes the bags on his way to the ring. The 23-year-old is one of just three fighters now under Billy Graham's tutelage: the trio being completed by Ricky's younger brother Matthew Hatton.

Macklin, a Birmingham lad of Irish parents, made the switch to Billy Graham's gym two years ago in a bid to boost both his training and profile. A dark, handsome, cheerful lad, he studied law at university before dropping out to pursue his boxing ambitions.

Ricky spots the day's new arrival, stops his shadow boxing routine and hangs out of the ropes.

"Here he is! Irish f****** champion? Never been to Ireland the ****!" He jokes.

Macklin smiles, then laughs as Hatton prolongs the abuse.

"Irish champion and you've never been to Ireland you Brummie w*****."

With that, Ricky flashes a few more left-right combinations at the offending mirror before climbing out of the ropes to hammer one of the heavy bags for three, three minute bursts. It's a joy to watch as he ducks and weaves before another right, then left, pounds the bag in one direction then the other.

Each time a punch lands it's greeted with the familiar Hatton guttural grunt…
"nnnnaaaaaarrrggghhhh!" It sounds like the bark of a demented dog suffering with a heavy cold.

"People ask if I feel like I made a mistake in leaving Frank. Are these people stupid? Earning more money, topping the bill in America, moving up a weight and challenging for these titles!"

"nnnnaaaaarrrggghhhh!"

1.30pm……

There's an extra spring in Ricky's step today. He lands one more left hook, then leaves the still swinging heavy bag to think about what it's done, and walks the ten yards to Billy's office.

Last night he had his first look at a video of Luis Collazo and now wants to share his thoughts with Billy Graham who's busy in his office tearing up cabbage leaves for Liston the Lizard's lunch.

Ricky weaves and flicks out jabs in a southpaw stance as he shows Billy what he saw Collazo doing on tape. The mind now very much focused on opponent rather than merely the date of the fight.

So, what is his early opinion of the WBA welterweight champ? "I've looked at the tapes a few times," he says as sweat drips from his soaking head, down his nose and onto the wooden floor. "He's a southpaw and very, very quick.

"He's bigger than me as I'm not a natural welterweight. I might go back to light-welter after the fight, but it's a good opportunity for me to get another title.

"Not a lot of people become a world champion, but to become a two-weight world champion will cement my place in British boxing history."

With that, it's back to the bag for a few more rounds, then on the pads, bags, bar and weights. Two hours later, over coffee in the Betta Bodies canteen, Ricky works through his day.

"Well, we're upping the training now and I've now started jumping the bar," he said. "Monday, Wednesday and Friday we're jumping the bar at the minute. This is the first week we've been working on the bar and I've gone straight in at six rounds rather than the four I'd normally do at this stage so I'm ahead of schedule.

"On the easy days – Tuesdays and Thursdays - I'll just go on the pads with Billy, working on technique. We push it Monday, Wednesday, Friday and on the other days we'll wind it down a bit and talk a bit about tactics. We discuss my opponent, stuff like that.

"We'll start off doing six rounds on the pads and work it up to 15 in the week up to the fight. I don't want to over cook it but I'll start stepping up from six to nine to 15 rounds, then on the body-belt with Billy. Later on we'll be getting some sparring partners in who're the mirror-image of my opponent.

"When I leave the gym, I'll go home and then go

running at about half-past seven. I'll do about five miles and start picking the pace up a little bit now. After the run, I'll come home and have a bath.

"Then I'll have my last meal of the day and my Pro-Recover [drink]. I'll watch a bit of TV then get in bed about half-ten. I put the TV on a timer and nod off when I nod off. But I feel fit already and there's seven and a half weeks to go!"

On the subject of running, in preparation for the Kostya Tszyu fight, Ricky had been training in the early hours of the morning to get his body ready for the 2am start at the MEN Arena – the time fixed to suit a US TV audience.

On one particular morning, the police had become suspicious of a young, hooded male tearing through the streets of Gee Cross, Hyde. There'd been a spate of robberies in the area, so they stopped what they thought was a hoodie thug.

"As soon as I turned around they noticed who I was," Ricky says. "They said, 'we should have known it was you, Ricky. What other idiot would be running at two in the morning?'

"But it wasn't as hard as people think. Instead of getting up at nine o'clock in the morning I was getting up at midday. Instead of getting to bed at midnight I'd go to bed at four in the morning. So really I just stayed in bed that little bit longer for the five weeks running up to the fight."

As far as training for the Collazo fight is concerned, he'll be sticking to civil hours. The fight is pencilled in for 10pm Boston time – this time of course, he'll be Stateside.

As ever, Ricky's diet and weight training schedule is being painstakingly monitored by his strength and nutrition coach Kerry Kayes. The step up to welterweight provides Kerry with a different challenge. He now has to prepare Ricky for the ten stone seven weight limit: shedding fat while gaining extra bulk.

Ricky's quite happy at the prospect of stepping up, "I wouldn't say it's been difficult, but I've always had to work to make light-welterweight. I'll be very big and strong at welterweight. In fact, my conditioning should be even better because I'm not having to deprive myself of food as much as I'd normally do. With the better nutrition and training, and with less weight to lose, I'll probably go into turbo charge."

"I'll have the usual six meals a day, but Kerry's added more protein into the diet and it'll be better this time because I've got half a stone less to lose. My definition will look bigger, I'll be doing more weight training and the nutrition side of it will be that little bit better.

"I haven't started going to my mum's for tea yet though. I do it myself at the moment as it isn't as extreme as if I was fighting at light-welter. About six weeks before the fight, I'll go to my mum's.

"It's easy at the minute. I take stuff home from the gym that Kerry makes up for me. Otherwise it's just pasta, chicken, fish, stuff that doesn't take much working out. My diet gets considerably better nearer the fight and I need the good fuel then for the energy.

"I'm going to stay and train here until about a week before the fight, and then I'll head over to the States. I'll give it plenty of time so I don't take any chances.

"But on the whole, everything's going well and its bang on track and from a fitness point of view I'm a little bit ahead of schedule.

"I've become the undisputed light-welter weight champion so let's now become a two-time champion. I'm fourth in the list of pound-for-pound fighters so hopefully I can become the best pound-for-pound fighter."

With the announcement of Luis Collazo as opponent and the step up a division, inevitably sections of the press are suggesting the transition is necessary because Ricky struggles to make the ten stone limit.

According to Team Hatton, making the weight has never been an issue, and the switch is simply tactical. Ricky is confident the media will eventually appreciate the risks he's prepared to take.

"I think I'll get huge applause because a lot of people have been saying for years that I've been ducking this guy and avoiding that guy.

"I beat Kostya Tszyu – the number two pound-for-pound best fighter on the planet. I beat him to become undisputed light-welterweight champion then went straight into a unification fight with Carlos Maussa.

"I beat him and took his belt and for my next fight, people might have expected me to take an easy touch but instead I'm making a step up in

"Not a lot of people become a world champion, but to become a two-weight world champion will cement my place in British boxing history."

The Preacher

Monday, 27 March......

Billy Graham is something of a Manchester boxing legend. A middleweight in his fighting days, he had 12 pro fights during the mid 1970s notching up ten wins – three by knockout – and two defeats. He's not, you imagine, very similar to his evangelical namesake.

At the age of 35 he was training in Phil Martin's Champs Camp gym in Manchester's Moss Side in a bid to get his professional fighter's licence back. That bid failed and he had to think again. He stayed on at the gym and fell into the training game where, much to his delight, he realised he could still get that boxing buzz by preparing fighters for battle.

The Preacher's 'George Best moment' came when, now based in Salford, a 17 year old scrawny little kid from Hyde walked into his gym. Billy reckons he felt like the Manchester United scout who spotted the Belfast boy. Ricky has been with him every step of the way since, moving on together to a gym in Hattersley, until they settled into the Kerry Kayes-owned Betta Bodies gym in Denton.

It's Billy's very own little world where he trains his three fighters. Along with Ricky there's Matthew Macklin and Matthew Hatton, light-middleweight and welterweight respectively. Obviously Ricky is the number one fighter in the gym, and while Billy doesn't favour any of the trio, Ricky inevitably gets priority.

A few weeks into training for the Collazo fight and the heavy work is now underway. Ricky has to get his weight down. He's currently around a stone and a half above the 10 stone 7 pounds limit, but all's going to plan and Billy has no problem with his fighter's off-training habits that lead to him needing to lose so much weight.

"Everybody has to wind down," he explains as he leans against the wall of the spartan Phoenix Camp office he shares with Liston, and lights up a Benson & Hedges.

"Being a fighter's a very traumatic business, know what I mean? It's an awful lot of pressure. He needs a bit of a comedown. Obviously I wish he wouldn't put so much weight on because it makes it harder for himself, but that's the animal he is.

"You can't fault him. He'll do anything - work really hard - and he's like a monk when he's training for a fight.

"The people that keep it steady all year round are the people that it isn't a sacrifice to. I've trained fighters who don't drink, don't want to go out, married with kids or whatever, so it's no sacrifice. But most fighters are extroverts so it comes with the territory.

"As long as it's right when it comes to the training I'm okay with it. He's successful isn't he? That's the way he likes to do it. Ricky's very sociable, he likes company and I like him the way he is."

Billy takes a drag of his cigarette and as he exhales he adds with a smile: "I just wish the fat bastard wouldn't put so much weight on!"

When training begins it's the same routine. A stretch, some shadow boxing, some skipping, working the bags and 'touching around' on the pads with Billy. On the easy days – Tuesdays and Thursdays – the pair will talk tactics.

"I like to look at tapes of the opponents as soon as possible and I like my fighters to look at the tapes. Some fighters don't like looking at the tapes because it makes them nervous. But I think you're better off knowing if the kid has a good left-hook or whatever. It's better to know what they're facing and know what angles and all that.

"He's still getting his weight down, he'll do weights, watch his diet and he's doing a bit of touching around in the ring with me. I like to get in and do a couple of sessions to make sure he's not rusty and still finding the angles. But it doesn't take much for him to get back into it.

"Next week we'll start on the body-belt, we'll do a few rounds together and generally build it up."

The famous 'body-belt'. Ricky's favourite. He gets to tear around a ring, pounding Billy for all he's worth. The belt, Billy's protection, is nine inches of foam encased with leather. When it's strapped on, the trainer looks like he's wearing a cross between an absurd oversized waistcoat and the top half of a sumo wrestler fat suit.

The sessions on the belt always draw a crowd. But it can be a painful business – even with the Preacher calling out for divine intervention from time to time.

"It's the bit I used to enjoy till I got older and got a load of injuries," Billy says. "A week before the fight we'll do 15 rounds with the belt and that's a killer!"

"Ricky's very sociable, he likes company and I like him the way he is. I just wish the fat bastard wouldn't put so much weight on!"

12.20pm......

He stubs out his cigarette, leaves the office and the lizard, and gets to work. Billy likes to stay in shape himself and the old habits die hard. Ten minutes of skipping is followed by some work on a speed ball in the far corner of the gym.

The Preacher's working up a sweat before Ricky arrives for his day's training. The affection Billy holds for his fighter is obvious. You get the impression that despite the rough edges, he has a soft side not just reserved for reptiles or snakes.

"I'd say anybody who wins titles is a bit special," Billy says as he rhythmically slaps the ball: two with the left, two with the right.

"I've been training Ricky since he was 17; he had his first pro fight at 18. He's had 40 fights and he's been busy. As well as that he's extremely talented.

"I've always worked with top fighters since my days at Champs Camp. There's never been a year when I haven't trained a champion fighter. He's just that little bit special. It was quite evident the first day I saw him.

"He's got exceptional balance, he's very strong for his weight and genetically he's got a wicked heart and lungs. So he's blessed with a lot of natural attributes but he's also blessed with a mind that can take things in.

"Some fighters you can talk to till the cows come home but they won't understand you. Rick's a student of the game."

12.40pm......

The student obviously does listen to his teacher, but whether or not he takes everything in is up for debate.

The Hitman's now arrived at the gym. So what of his trainer's influence?
Feeling mischievous, Ricky recounts the story of his fight with tough American Vince Phillips in April 2003. At the time Phillips was the only man to have beaten Kostya Tszyu.

"That fight taught me so much it was unbelievable 'cos from the second round onwards I thought I had him out of there," Ricky says. "At the

end of the second round, Billy in the corner says, 'get on top of him; get to the body, right hand, left hook. He's knackered, jump on him!'" Ricky laughs, then gets animated as he continues.

"After round five Billy says, 'he's f****d Rick, get on top of him, right hand, get to the body, jump on him now!'

"Round seven, round eight, he says, 'he's knackered Rick, his legs are going, jump on him, get on top of him, he's f****d!'

"Round nine, Billy says, 'he's knackered, his legs are gone, get to the body, right hand, left hook, jump all over him!'

"Round ten, round eleven, he says, 'he's knackered Rick, jump on top of him!' I said, 'Billy – f*** off! You've been saying that since nine o'clock, it's now quarter to ten!'"

Ricky won with a wide points margin that night.

Back to Billy, and not surprisingly for a man who found his true vocation purely by chance, his training methods at the Phoenix Camp Gym differ from other gyms.

"I have quite a lot of my own methods, know what I mean?"

He's about to elaborate but is distracted by his mobile phone ringing back in the office. He makes a dash and gets there in time. It was Matthew Macklin's dad Seamus just saying hello. He gets back in the groove.

"It's seems like I've been training forever. I have one fight, then another fight. I look after myself physically," he says with no sense of irony as he reaches for another B&H, "especially since I got older.

"Maybe other trainers don't spend as much time in the gym as me, or do the same amount on the body belt as I do. I spend an awful lot of time with my fighters and have done since day one.

"I've trained intensely for title fights all through the weights and it's really given me an insight into how to break someone up. I think I'm pretty good at that.

"The body-belt helps recreate what's gonna go on in the ring and it helps cut down on sparring. I probably don't do as much sparring as other trainers. The only reason I can get away with that is because I'm on the body-belt so much. It's worked for me over the years.

"I used to spar too much. I was a big believer, but I've learned it's wrong. I'm not scared to change. I like to bring in modern methods. Some don't work.

"I've always been big into weights. It's been frowned upon by the boxing fraternity for years, which is complete nonsense. In fact, I refuse to train a boxer who won't train on the weights."

Boxers lifting weights is still a point of contention. Traditionalists argue that it reduces mobility, a case usually backed up by pointing to Frank Bruno as an example. The big heavyweight was a phenomenal specimen to look at, but he certainly wasn't the quickest.

"The argument is nonsense," Billy says succinctly. "They've been looking at bodybuilders and their exaggerated physiques and obviously that would affect mobility. But boxers don't use weights for that: you use them so you can be as strong as you can possibly be, pound-for-pound. And it'll make you faster – not slower.

"I'm a boxing man, but I'm not afraid to bring experts in. I brought Kerry Kayes in because he's an expert in nutrition.

"But there are other things I do. My fighters don't run in the mornings, they run in the evenings. There's a big thing about fighters running in the morning, which is nonsense. There's so many clichés about boxing.

"We're not nocturnal; we're not supposed to be up at the crack of dawn when the body wants to rest. Then you've got to come back and go to bed so you go through the process twice. Then they come into the gym a little bit jaded.

"I like my fighters to come into the gym fresh and alert so I can work on some technical stuff. Also, if a fighter's had his run in the morning, then comes into the gym, what's he going to do in the evening? Sit around and think about food. Running in the evening breaks up the night.

"I also do hard days and easy days because I understand the body's recovery. I'm no soft taskmaster, but the body has to rebuild and repair and rest. You can't kill it every day. You wouldn't think of over-training a muscle every day, so what's the difference with the heart? That's a muscle – it's a pump! You've got to rest a little bit."

Along with the different methods, there's a unique atmosphere evident at the Phoenix Camp, an openness to Billy's gym seldom found elsewhere. Punters can, and do, walk in off the street to have a look at the boxers training.

"Some gyms like to do things behind closed doors," he says. "I'm not like that. As soon as I got my own gym I was happy for people to drop in and have a cup of tea. It has its drawbacks, but making a gym inaccessible is too big a price to pay.

"Anyone can see what we're all about here. We're dedicated, but you don't have to walk around with a stern face all the time. You know, it's easy and loose and that's the way I like it. Just because we mess about doesn't mean we're not serious.

"A lot of trainers are sergeant-major types and that's fair enough. Some fighters might need that, but if they do, then stay away from me. You either do what you've gotta do to be successful, or I'll just ignore you!

"I don't know how many champions I've trained – well over 90 – so I've always made a living out of boxing. I'm making big money now, know what I mean? but I've always made a living."

With only three boxers, the camp is small and unified. They all work closely together and being the senior fighter, Ricky is constantly chipping in, giving advice and tips to the other two. Today he's showing Matthew Macklin a shot he's been working on: a left hook, left uppercut combination.

Ricky has ambitions of becoming a trainer when he steps outside the ring.

"Fighters learn an awful lot by watching other fighters," Billy says. "I think it helps. Matthew Macklin has a lot of similar things in his game plan as Ricky. They're different shapes, but Matthew also likes to go to the body as well and they're both predators.

"I don't mind input and comments from any of my fighters, but not from anybody else thank you!

"I encouraged Ricky to get his second's licence almost immediately after he turned pro because I wanted him to feel the atmosphere of a big fight night.

"He's actually a good cornerman. He's helped me quite a few times. In fact he once had to be my chief second when I had to go to hospital when I had a piece of steak stuck in my stomach. I knew I could trust Ricky, particularly as it was his brother fighting at the time.

"I've always liked to have my fighters in the corner. We're like a team and I like that."

A Bitch of a Day

Tuesday, 28 March......

11.30am......

It's being reported today that Ricky's domestic rival Junior Witter is to fight DeMarcus Corley for the vacant WBC light-welterweight title, a belt given up by Floyd Mayweather Jnr.

Three-weight world champion Mayweather is to step up to face IBF welterweight champion Zab Judah on 8 April.

Witter is due to defend his European title first against Giuseppe Lauri, before getting a shot at Corley in July.

Never short of throwing a few words in Ricky's direction, the Bradford fighter is quoted as saying: "If we were both world champions, I still don't know if Hatton would face me, even though it would be the biggest fight in British boxing history.

"I was offered to his American broadcasters HBO and I hear they approved me. But instead of taking me on and giving everyone the fight they want to see, he is looking elsewhere."

Ricky looks utterly bored by the news and simply shrugs his shoulders. He's not interested in responding, but eventually shares his thoughts.

"There's every chance a fight with Witter won't happen now," he says. "Junior Witter could have the WBC belt, the IBF belt, the WBA belt, but he's got no style and he's got no charisma.

"He doesn't sell tickets. He can have all the belts and still no one will give a shit about him.

"Junior Witter's paid his due, you know he's got a British and Commonwealth title and if he can win a world title then fair play to him, but he's been shouting his mouth off for years.

"I've beaten Kostya Tszyu, the undisputed champion, and Carlos Maussa to win the WBA belt. I'm *The Ring* magazine's fighter of the year, the British Board of Boxing Control's fighter of the year and I'm stepping up a weight to try and become welterweight champion and then people ask me about Junior Witter!

"It might happen, but to be honest I'd much sooner fight Mayweather or Cotto. I've just signed a deal with HBO while Junior Witter's fighting European and British fighters. It's not going to appeal to a HBO audience so I can't really see it happening. He stands a better chance if he wins that title and he should do. He'll beat Corley I think."

Midday......

If Ricky has been needled by the Witter story, his day isn't getting any better. He's found out he'll definitely have to give up his IBF crown after refusing to fight their mandatory challenger Naoufel Ben Rabah.

The Hitman's been forced to ditch the belt he won by stopping the legendary Kostya Tszyu, so he can pursue a more lucrative, defining fight with Luis Collazo. Even so, he's disappointed.

"I have a great relationship with the IBF and they understand why I couldn't go through with a mandatory defence against Rabah.

"But you know, this is an opportunity to become champion in another division and I don't think it'd be difficult to get a shot at any of the belts should I come back down to light-welterweight.

"There'll be further career-defining fights for me, and with all due respect to Rabah he cannot be counted among the big names.

"In an ideal world I'd like to keep all the belts but that isn't possible in this day and age.

"The IBF belt means a lot to me, because I won it against Kostya Tszyu, which makes it a massive prize. But once I had signed for the Collazo fight, Rabah's people did a double shuffle and told the IBF that their man wants to fight for it now.

"Fortunately I've still got the WBA light-welterweight title and after beating Tszyu I've become the universally recognised number one in the division. No matter what belt I hold now, if you want to be the man at light-welterweight, you have to beat me. Even if I was to vacate all the belts.

"It upsets me a bit, but HBO didn't want me to make a mandatory defence."

Billy Graham isn't feeling so diplomatic: "I'm not too pleased with the IBF; I'm not too pleased with HBO and I'm not too pleased with some other things.

"But everyone knows who the light-welterweight champion of the world is. It's Ricky Hatton, and it still will be now they've stripped him of the belt. I'm not concerned.

"I didn't want him (Collazo) as Ricky's next opponent, but I've got over that now and I've no doubts he'll beat him. It's all about looking good in America, but I've got my head on now and I'm feeling good.

"I want to state that Ricky Hatton is still the light-welterweight champion of the world and that this fight at welterweight is a one-off fight. I don't want anyone to forget that."

The Guru

1.45pm......

For the average nine-to-fiver, the lunch hour is a sacred time to escape the humdrum mediocrity of a working life spent in an office, factory or wherever. Kerry Kayes uses his time-out each day to get a world champion into shape.

A former national bodybuilding champion, Kerry is a nutrition and fitness expert and the man behind the Phoenix Camp's diet and strength programme. Every day at around 1pm, Kerry leaves the office at his Denton factory and heads over to the gym to supervise preparations.

Always open to new ideas, Billy Graham realised bodybuilders and boxers could work together, and invited Kerry into the team in 2002, after setting up camp in a room at the back of the latter's Betta Bodies gym.

"Whether you like bodybuilding or not, you've got to respect that bodybuilders are experts at losing weight healthily," says Kerry. "It's important that a boxer loses weight before he steps on the scales, but also retains as much muscle as possible.

"If you do without food evenly, i.e. carbs, proteins and fats, the body will cannibalise fat but it will also cannibalise muscle. So what we've got to do is retain as much muscle as we can. In bodybuilding you do that for a visual effect, in boxing and other sports you do it for power and strength."

When Kerry was competing on the bodybuilding circuit he realised there weren't enough nutritional products available to help bodybuilders, so he went into business. CNP Professional supplements are now sold in 27 countries and are very much a part of the Phoenix boxers' diets.

In his Betta Bodies gym, pictures of Kerry in his bodybuilding pomp line the walls. Meeting him today, his past wouldn't be strikingly evident. A short, bespectacled man in his fifties, wearing jeans and a t-shirt, he doesn't look particularly muscle-bound. There's even the slight beginnings of a middle-aged spread.

Kerry has a cheery demeanour with a ready laugh and enjoys an obvious rapport with the fighters. They listen when he talks.

"At first I had to tread very carefully with the boxers. I arrived and I had to say to world champions, 'right, this is nothing to do with boxing, its weight management and you're doing everything wrong'.

"For Ricky's first fight I stepped back and probably only did about 30 percent of what I wanted to do. I increased it a bit for the second fight.

"The most glaring problem was that they were not drinking: they were not taking in fluids. There's this 'no-no' in boxing that if you drink water you'll put on weight, but there are no calories in water. So the first thing I had to do was get them drinking two litres a day. Now, they'll drink eight litres a day.

"The other thing is that they weren't eating. A boxer, when he has to make the weight, thinks the best way to do it – and remember these are incredibly strong-willed men who can overcome hunger – is by not eating. But by not eating, your metabolism slows down and your body holds on to everything. The best way to lose weight is to eat small and often.

"From food, I moved on to specific nutrients. When you're training, you're breaking your body down so it has to recover. So we have specific pro-recovery drinks and extra protein in supplements and vitamins and minerals. It probably took about 18 months to get them doing exactly what I wanted."

Kerry is sitting on the ring apron when his mobile goes off. Appropriately, he has the theme tune to Peter Kay's *Phoenix Nights* on his phone. He finishes his call and the subject switches to Ricky, his weight and off-training habits.

"I've worked with many athletes in many sports and I've found that the more disciplined the athlete, the quicker they tend to burn out believe it or not," he explains.

"There are two scenarios. There's the physical scenario and the mental scenario. The pressure Ricky's under is awesome so I think he is the type of person who has to get out of shape to get into shape. Mentally it's positive, physically it sometimes takes its toll on his body but he's always in great shape for his fights.

"I think Billy summed it up when he told Ricky, 'you're not using Kerry, you're abusing Kerry'. He thought because I was helping him, he could get a little more out of shape."

Billy hears this as he walks past and with a big grin across his face chips in, "I wish I had everyone doing everything wrong like him. Know what I mean?"

Kerry lets out a loud cackle, then continues: "It's a big story about Ricky Hatton's weight control. But at every fight everyone talks about the phenomenal condition he's in. This next fight up is at welterweight and it's been taken for specific, tactical reasons, but they'll all say it's because he can't make light-welter!

"The only reason Ricky will ever have to move up to welter is if he chooses to for tactical reasons. From a body composition point of view Ricky can stay at light-welter for the rest of his career."

Ricky's in the ring now, moving around after Billy who has the pads on. Trainer, all wide-eyed, calls the shots as fighter throws an uppercut with such force he's off his feet. Each blow is accompanied with the familiar grunt and fierce expression – terrible intent in the Hitman's narrow sunken eyes and he's only 'touching around' with his mate.

The extra weight Ricky carried into the gym on his first day back in training is shifting quickly.

"From day one of Ricky's training he is a Buddhist monk." Kerry says. "He's probably that pissed off with eating shit and drinking Guinness he puts a date in the diary and that's it.

"For the first couple of weeks he actually eats

more food than he has been doing because he's been so slack, just eating the odd Chinese and the odd pizza. He definitely gets more nutrients. There are case studies of grossly overweight people who are malnourished because they're getting empty calories and no nutrients.

"I'm here as a safety valve now. Ricky knows what he's doing and he's a clever lad. He can easily lose five or six pounds from his first week's training because a lot of it is fluid retention from bad food, all the preservatives and other stuff he's been eating.

"We want him to eat five meals a day. He'll have one or two pro-recovery meals. It's sachet form mixed with water probiotics.

"Now, eight weeks before a fight, he'll have a blend of amino acids, which will help repair the muscles. That has to be taken on an empty stomach. All the lads notice an increase in strength within a week of taking that.

"Then he'll take pro-vital, which is a mixture of vitamins, minerals and nutrients. This is a bit of an insurance policy. If you're eating a clean, healthy diet you won't need it, but if you boil your veg a bit too long you lose nutrients and I can't rely on the lads to eat enough vegetables because they don't like them. I also make sure he takes all his fatty acid supplements – omega threes and sixes.

"His clean diet is chicken breast, broccoli, runner beans, pasta and potatoes. We're also increasing his protein, as muscle is stored protein."

Along with his dietary needs, Kerry also acts as strength coach for the Phoenix fighters. For this fight, Ricky will be doing more weightlifting than ever before.

"What we want now is Ricky at ten stone seven with a bit more muscle so we'll do a bit more with the weights. But I always remember that the weightlifting is to supplement his boxing, not to make him a weightlifter, so I have to do the weightlifting with one arm tied behind me back. I've also got to be very careful about injuries."

There's always been a fine line between success and failure in sport but with the demands of boxing, and the rewards on offer at the very top of the game, every tiny advantage a fighter can gain through diet and fitness is explored by Kerry. He's particularly proud of the influence his strength work has had on the fighters.

"Boxers don't lift weights because of old wives' tales from the past. Now, I know that Ricky Hatton would feel he hadn't prepared properly if he didn't lift weights.

"Don't forget, only ten or 15 years ago footballers didn't lift weights. Look at the weightlifting rooms at football grounds. Boxing and football are explosive sports. If you have a stronger muscle it's gonna explode faster. Simple as that. You can't reinvent the wheel!

"In an ideal world we do the weights every day bar Wednesday, which is a rest day. So Monday we'll do quadriceps, which is the front thighs and calfs; Tuesday we'll do chest and biceps; Thursday we'll do back and hamstrings and on Friday we'll do shoulders and triceps.

"I never get Ricky in the bodybuilding gym until after his boxing, so he's already a little bit spent. I stop the weightlifting two weeks before a fight.

"Billy puts Ricky through two hard weeks of training near the fight and then the last week is rest.

"Boxers don't lift weights because of old wives' tales from the past. Now, I know that Ricky Hatton would feel he hadn't prepared properly if he didn't lift weights. If you have a stronger muscle it's gonna explode faster. Simple as that."

Kerry Kayes

The first hard week I do weights, the second hard week it'd be too much.

"He only does about 20 minutes' weightlifting each session. But it's proper weightlifting where the muscles fail and that's the only way you can get stronger.

"The biggest tightrope I walk is injury because Ricky's a naturally strong lad who can lift. On the leg presses he can lift more than some of the bodybuilders. Ricky's got a short leverage so he's strong, and some of his fights are 20 percent wrestling if you think about it, so they can feel his strength. The downside is, the stronger he gets, the greater the worry of injury.

"I won't let him lift free-weights even though they're better than machines. I make sure he's properly warmed up, and on some movements I don't let him fully extend so as to save pressure on his knees and ankles."

Conversation over, Kerry gives Ricky the nod and the pair of them head off to pump some iron.

Ricky's Diets

(Pic. Paul Speak)

Non-Training Day

Breakfast

11.00am

Mega-breakfast (Butty Box, Hyde) - three
sausages, three rashers of bacon, two eggs, hash
browns, black pudding, baked beans, grilled
tomatoes and two slices of toast.
Coffee with two sugars.

Lunch

2.00pm

Fish and chips.
Can of Coke.

Dinner

7.00pm

Chicken Madras, pilau rice, naan bread.
Two pints of lager.

Snack

10.00pm

Packet of pork scratchings.
Eight pints of Guinness.

Ricky's typical diet
Training Day

Breakfast

10.30am

Pro GF (Growth Factors) – a blend of nutrients specifically designed to enhance strength, recuperation and stamina. Best taken on an empty stomach.
- 2 scoops of formula mixed in a pint of water.

11.00am

Pro MR (Meal Replacement) – a high protein meal replacement supplement containing a blend of fast and slow un-denatured proteins creating a steady release of amino acids into the bloodstream for muscle growth and repair.
- One sachet mixed in a pint of water.

Pro Vital – high strength vitamin and mineral formula.
- 4 capsules and 1 tablet.

Pro Lipid – a blend of essential fatty acids, omega 3,6,9.
- 5 capsules.

Porridge – if he fancies it.

Lunch

2.45pm

Pro Recover – a blend of fast-acting proteins and glucose polymers consumed immediately after intense exercise to maximise recovery.

3.15pm

Clean Meal – chicken or fish, green vegetables, potatoes, rice or pasta.

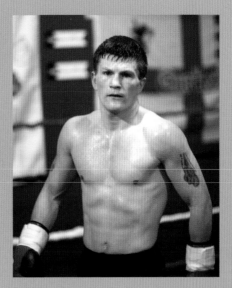

Snack

6.00pm

Pro Flapjack – low in saturated fat and simple sugars, high in quality protein.

Dinner

8.00pm

Pro Recover.

Clean Meal or Pro MR (Meal Replacement).

Pro Vital – *1 tablet, 1 capsule.*

Pro Lipid – *5 capsules.*

Snack

10.00pm

Pro Flapjack.

CNP Professional (Chemical Nutritional Products),

The Two Matthews

In the Red corner……

12.40pm……

It can't be easy trying to make a name for yourself in the unforgiving sport of boxing when your stablemate is your brother, who also happens to be Ricky 'the Hitman' Hatton, an undisputed world champion.

But Matthew 'Magic' Hatton isn't fazed by the unfair pressure. He's his own man and is finding his feet as a welterweight on his own terms. An indication of his strength of character can be found in the football team he follows. Despite growing up in a household of staunch Manchester City supporters, Matthew stands alone in his devotion to United.

"I was born with a little more sense than the others," he says with a straight face. "They're all gluttons for punishment. Everyone presumes we're all Blues, but no, I'm a Red.

"When we used to live in a pub in Hattersley, I was only maybe six years old at the time and just starting to get into football. One of the regulars gave me a Manchester United badge. A tiny, farty little badge. But I started to watch United then and got taken to a couple of games so that was that.

"We do enjoy the rivalry, especially on derby day, although I'm not too pleased about this season."

No doubt Ricky made the most of the fact his team have taken four points off United in their two meetings this term.

Matthew has arrived early for training, which is staggered so Billy can give each fighter the attention they need.

Hatton junior is slightly taller than his sibling and has a leaner, more wiry frame. His dress sense isn't much different though: black baseball cap pulled down over his eyes, a black Londsdale t-shirt and tracksuit bottoms. White trainers complete the outfit.

His face is softer than Ricky's, his nose less visibly damaged by ring-war, but there's the same Hatton steeliness in narrow eyes as he answers the inevitable question about being in his brother's shadow.

"It's not too much of a hindrance to me," he says with a shake of the head. "It's a question I get asked a lot. But as long as I'm being the best that I can be then that's all that matters.

"Ricky's helped me a lot in my career. We've done a lot of sparring and he gives me a lot of tips.

"I don't put any undue pressure on myself by looking at what he's doing; I just concentrate on what I'm doing. Now things are coming good and I'm starting to make a name for myself.

"This time next year, hopefully if I get that British title, people will know who I am."

Matthew's working week in the build-up to a fight is basically the same as Ricky's, if a little less intense as he is preparing for an eight-round fight (rather than 12) on the undercard of the Hatton v Collazo fight. The opponent is as yet unknown.

With only three fighters remaining under Billy Graham's watch, 'Magic' has benefited from the extra attention – a fact underlined by his performance in stopping his last opponent earlier in the month, the Belarusian Alexander Abramenko.

"Things are going great at the minute. I'm finding my own style now. My last performance in Monte Carlo was one of my best and I now feel I'm coming into my own."

"I still feel as though I'm an undefeated fighter. One of the fights I lost – and it's not just me saying this – was a really bad decision. Everyone thought I'd won.

"The other fight was stopped because of a cut eye when I was winning, and winning comfortably. With a little bit of luck it would have been 30 and 0 now.

"When I lost on a cut that was the first time I'd been cut. I did go through a period where I got cut in quite a few fights, and I thought, 'will I have the same problem as Ricky!' But I've altered my style a bit and I've not been cut since."

The younger Hatton turned professional at 19 after just 22 amateur fights. Now 24, he's done the vast majority of his learning and growing in the professional game.

"Early on I did get a bit frustrated because I knew the talent that I had and I wasn't producing it in the ring. But that was due to inexperience and people that see me fight now, who maybe saw me fight three years ago, don't recognise me. It's all down to experience.

"By Christmas time I want to be fighting for the British title. I'm ready for that step now. I feel I'm one of the best welterweights in the country. I've had 30 fights and I'm ready to prove that. I'm ranked 7th in the country so I'm ready for the step."

As is the Team Hatton/Phoenix Camp ethic, all the fighters support the others. If one of the trio has a fight, they're all in the corner.

"Ricky's got a lot of experience in the fight game, but obviously Billy's the main man in the corner giving advice. But Ricky puts his little bit in. He helps me out and gives me good advice.

"We get on well as brothers. We go out together, have a drink together and we have a good laugh and a lot of banter as well.

"Ricky's obviously moving up to welterweight for his next fight but we'd never box each other. My dad's got a few grey hairs already, but that would turn him white overnight!

"We do a lot of sparring together but that's obviously different. When you get in the ring on the night, you're getting in there to get your opponent whichever way you can. There's no way you can fight your brother."

Matthew straightens up after leaning against the wall next to one of the big windows on the right-hand-side of the gym. He picks up his kit bag and heads for the changing room. As he walks past the heaviest bag en-route, he can't resist throwing a quick left-hook.

In the Green corner......

The double doors at the front of the gym open once more. Whoever's about to come in is still talking to someone on the other side – their identity hidden in the dark of the non-lit entrance. With the doors open, a glorious burst of fresh air whistles into the purposely stifling gym.

Standing around in this place with all the radiators on full-blast is bad enough; contemplating any form of exercise seems faintly ridiculous. But it's hot because that's how Ricky likes it.

Unfortunately the doors close once more to seal the Phoenix Camp sauna. The entrant is Matthew Macklin. He wears a huge, sparkling-white, toothy grin as he greets Billy, who is shadow boxing in the ring.

Matthew takes a seat on the ring apron as Billy bounces away on the canvas a few feet away.

His white t-shirt has a picture of himself on it with 'Champion Macklin' printed in bold. There's no-one quite like a boxer when it comes to self-promotion, although Matt's personality is far from brash or cocky. He's polite and affable and enjoying life at the Phoenix Camp.

"Well I've trained in Freddie Roach's gym three or four times for a few weeks at a time and it's wicked. But this gym is the best," he says. "We're all mates here; it's quite close knit. We're all there for each other.

"We're all friends, but when we spar, we spar, there are no punches pulled. No bad intentions, but you're not doing anyone any favours if you do it half-hearted."

A world class amateur, the 23 year old's professional career has been dogged by injury and inactivity. He flew through his first seven fights before a broken hand hampered his progress. When he should have been fighting six or seven times a year, he could only manage two or three bouts

With his fitness regained, he then suffered another blow with a points defeat in November 2003 – when fighting for the English light-middleweight title against Andrew Facey – his only defeat in 17.

Frank Warren, who was promoting Macklin at the time, suggested a move to Manchester in a bid to get his career back on track.

"I think the Facey fight was a bad decision on the

night, but had I not had that loss I wouldn't have come here," he says. "It helped me make some adjustments to my training and Billy's a great trainer. It's also meant I've been sparring with Ricky."

On the subject of sparring, Matthew has now had the dubious pleasure of sharing the ring on countless afternoons with the Hitman. So what about those left hooks to the body and evil uppercuts?

"It's funny, when boxers say 'he never hurt me', they don't mean they weren't in pain, they mean they weren't rocking on their feet or winded." Matt explains. "He's never winded me, but I wouldn't say he hasn't hurt me!

"He's given me many a black eye and he's busted my nose up a few times! And there've been a couple of shots that have whizzed past the ribs and I've thought..... 'oooh I'm glad that missed!'

"Fortunately I've got the best part of a stone, if not a full stone on him when we spar and, you know, I'm pretty competent myself so I give as good as I get. But you don't realise how good he is until you get in there with him.

"I've always been a massive fan anyway, watching him from the outside. But he looks more vulnerable watching him on telly and you think you could catch him with this and that. You don't take into account how good his anticipation is, his reflexes and everything.

"That's why so many people made him such an underdog against Kostya Tszyu. But all those that were around him, we all fancied him. Maybe it was a bit of bias, but we knew how good he was. We knew all his strengths.

"Sometimes what makes a fighter special is something subtle. It's the subtleties, and that's what they [critics] were missing. People don't realise what a good boxer he is.

"Billy's a wicked trainer, and that's the main thing, but sparring with Ricky Hatton has brought me on leaps and bounds. He's not selfish. After a spar, he'll say do this, do that. He'll get you on the bags and talk. He tries to give you good pointers.

"He's down to earth. I didn't really know him before, but I'm sure he hasn't changed at all."

After claiming the Irish middleweight title in May 2005, Matthew boxed, and won, in Atlantic City and Philadelphia, building up Irish-American support in the process, before returning to England.

"A lot of people thought I'd jumped on the Irish bandwagon but that's not the case with me. I'd played hurling for Tipperary under-14s and I was gonna move back there when I was 14. I spent nine weeks there every summer holiday.

"Winning the Irish title was a big deal. Michael Monaghan, who I beat, has got a 16 and 16 record or something. But he has still been in with some good kids. He's had some tough tests. He boxed anyone at any notice and he said to me when we were having a drink in Ireland after the fight that I was the best kid he'd boxed. He'd boxed the likes of Carl Froch so that was a real confidence boost."

In his last fight on the Hatton v Maussa undercard, Matt made light work of a Russian prospect nicknamed 'Ferocious'. It didn't quite go according to plan for Alexey Chrikov who was ferociously knocked out in the first round. He had beaten former world champion Julio Cesar Vasquez and the manner of victory put Matt back in the spotlight.

The Irishman with the soft Brummie accent now has a shot at the British light-middleweight title when he takes on the champion, Salford's Jamie Moore in June.

1.25pm......

Ricky's milling around the gym now in his familiar all-black sweatsuit. In between rounds on the bag, he's hurling insults in the direction of all around him. While he takes a break to slug down some water, the subject of Moore v Macklin comes up.

"I'm close to all the lads in the gym and this is a difficult position for me to be in because the lad Matthew's boxing, Jamie, has been a friend of mine since I was 13 years of age. If I had my choice I

wouldn't like them to fight each other as they're both my mates.

"But it'll be the domestic fight of the year. It won't be one for the faint hearted and it won't go the distance. It's a shame really 'cos one of them could end up getting knocked out. Obviously they're gonna fight each other, they're both champions, and they both want to further their careers.

"From my point of view though, it won't be nice to watch. Good luck to the pair of 'em."

Ricky grabs his water bottle and takes a good slug. Nothing unusual in that, except that he has an ulterior motive. He's spotted his solicitor Gareth Williams walk through the double doors.

Gareth, kitted out in a smart, light grey suit and blue shirt, is having a chat with one of the punters at the side of the ring. Ricky walks over with a straight face and holds out his hand. Gareth says,

"you alright Rick?" and touches his mitt. Ricky, now up close if not quite at eye contact with his tall solicitor, spits a good mouthful of water straight into Gareth's face.

"You little shit!" he says laughing as Ricky wheels away in delight. Water is, by now, all down the front of Gareth's shirt. He looks like he's stepped in off the street after being caught in one of Manchester's famous downpours.

With that, Ricky's quickly back in the mood as he bounds across the dark, worn, wooden floorboards to continue his assault on an offending punch bag.

3.20pm......

Why would somebody do such a thing and spit water in the face of another human, even if he is a solicitor?

"I'm a bit of a practical joker me," Ricky explains. "A lot of people in the past have said I don't take my fighting seriously. As they've got to know me they realise I'm a deadly serious person.

"Even though I might make jokes and mess about I'm not going to lose focus about the job in hand. It's just how I deal with it."

Friday, 31 March......

12.45pm......

Nearly five weeks of training completed and Ricky's feeing good. Any disappointment he may feel about losing the IBF belt isn't evident, and he knows better than anybody that present-day boxing is more about fights than titles.

He saunters into the gym to begin his session. The sun is shining outside and life is good. The mental effects of not having to lose those precious extra seven pounds are obviously having an impact.

"I'm about 12 pound off my fighting weight which is a massive luxury so my diet is fantastic. It's got to the stage now where I don't even have to worry about my weight. I could pretty much eat what I want now. So it's a luxury I've never really been able to afford.

"The training's going well, I start on the body-belt next week and I'll be getting sparring partners in about a fortnight's time."

Billy and Ricky have had a couple of discussions about who to bring in. It's a tricky task finding sparring partners for Ricky. They never tend to have

a great deal of fun. When he's facing an orthodox opponent, the two Matthews, and others oblige.

"This time the sparring partners are obviously going to be southpaws and I do have a couple of people in mind. I'll be contacting them in the next week," Ricky says. "They'll be fighters I've seen fight who are as near as possible in style as my opponent."

Apart from the step up in weight, Billy Graham hasn't been over enamoured with the prospect of his 'kid' fighting a tricky southpaw on his headlining US debut.

Ricky agrees it'll be tough, but his record against the unorthodox is good: "I've never lost to one, amateur or pro," he says. "They tend to be tricky for the first two or three rounds, until you get used to them.

"There aren't a lot of southpaws around, the majority of fighters are orthodox, so it makes it difficult. But I've never lost to one. They might give me a bit of a headache in the early rounds but then I get to grips with them."

But is there a bigger risk of getting cut or marked early on if it takes a few rounds to get used to a fighter's style?

"Well I'm moving up a weight as well so there's an extra half a stone on the end of every punch, so while you're getting used to the southpaw style you might have to take one or two shots until you get your timing and find your range. It's about damage limitation for the early rounds and then you step up a gear."

2.50pm......

After a typical session of bag work, 'touching around' on the pads, jumping the bar, 20 minutes of weights directed by Kerry and a stint on a stepper, Ricky's finished his business at the Phoenix. He still has his run to look forward to, but after he's showered and changed it's time to relax with a brew with his mates in the gym canteen.

It always takes a while before Ricky can actually sit down. Usually there are around eight to ten lads with their dads who want a picture with the champ and an autograph. The focus of their attention always does what is asked of him with no fuss. He's happy to pose for photos, always puts his arm around the kids and gives the camera a big cheesy grin.

"I'm more than happy to do it," he says genuinely. "All the success and the fame and money that goes with it isn't worth a thing if your own people think you're a dickhead."

Something for the Weekend

Friday, 31 March......

3.05pm......

Eventually Ricky takes his seat for the now tepid coffee (two sugars when not in training; none when in the monastery) sitting in front of him.

Apart from pounding the pavements for an evening run, Saturdays and Sundays are usually days to take it easy and let the body recover. But this weekend, Ricky's going to be busy.

His friend, the boxer Jane Couch has roped him into speaking at a testimonial dinner for Bristol City goalkeeper Steve Phillips on Saturday night. Then on Sunday he's the guest thrower on TV's *Bullseye* – the 'comeback kid' of darts shows.

"I've got six and a half weeks to go till the fight and I'm not at the extremely intense stage of the training yet. I'll do another fortnight of doing stuff like this and then I'll probably have to knock it on the head. Sometimes when you're working hard in the gym you need to have your feet up instead of running here, there and everywhere.

"Doing charity bits and all that is as much of my job as boxing, but as the fight gets nearer I'll do less and less.

"At the moment it's a break from the gym. It's a very boring life being a boxer when you're in training. You get up and eat; you go to the gym then you eat; you go running and eat and then go to bed. That's it basically, so sometimes it's nice to go to the odd function just to get away from the gym and the hard grind. In another month's time though, when it's really intense, when I've finished in the gym I won't feel like doing anything."

The Bristol gig was always going to be a bit too tempting for Ricky 'the Hitman' Hatton once he realised his sporting pals Paul 'Gazza' Gascoigne, Phil 'the Power' Taylor and Jimmy 'Whirlwind' White would also be there.

"I've got to know Gazza and Five Bellies quite well over the last few years," says the Hitman. "Gazza was an entertainer, one of the most gifted footballers we've had, certainly in the last 20 years. It'll be good to see him. He texts me and phones me from time to time and it's nice to see that with the rough ride that he's had, he's coming through the other end and looking better for it.

"Phil Taylor's been my mate now for a good number of years. He's a great, great bloke, and so is Jimmy White although I'm not that into snooker.

"Jane Couch is also a good friend of mine, the former world ladies boxing champion. She has the mean streak you need as a boxer, but you couldn't meet a nicer lady.

"It makes all the hard work worthwhile when you can be on first name terms with all these people. Because of the success I've had in the ring it means I can rub shoulders with these people. It's nice."

The invitation to appear on the cult classic *Bullseye* has come at a price: filming at Yorkshire TV in Leeds on Sunday afternoon clashes with Manchester City's home tie with Middlesbrough. Blessed relief some might argue (when not in the presence of a City fanatic/world boxing champion).

"I missed Chelsea away and I had a sportsman's dinner the night we played West Ham in the Cup. It's just unfortunate that it's a very, very busy time for me and although I'd love to be cheering the Blues on, certain things sometimes take precedence.

"I play darts for my local pub team on a Thursday night in Hattersley. I've always been a big darts fan and I play for the New Inn in the Hyde and Denton district darts league. I can throw a mean dart and I certainly win a lot more than I lose.

"I don't think I could change my profession to darts, although I could probably match the darts players in the drinking department!

"It never ceases to amaze me that because of what I've achieved in boxing, I'm invited on TV game shows that I used to watch and love as a kid like *A Question of Sport*, *They Think It's All Over* and *Bullseye*. I feel like I'm drunk half the time! You have to pinch yourself!

"I'll be throwing for the bronze bully. I've got to throw 301 or more with nine darts. It's difficult, but I'm capable of doing it. Very few do it though. As long as I don't make a dick of myself, and I get a good score!

"I wouldn't mind one of those little rubber Bullys and a tankard. That'd be awesome. I'll stick that in my kitchen."

Saturday, 1 April......

Six weeks to fight-night (no joke)......

Gee Cross, Hyde......

9am......

Ricky's friend/assistant/right-hand-man Paul Speak – or Speaky – is feeling lonesome. He's banging on the door of 'Heartbreak Hotel' but Elvis isn't home. After several minutes Ricky opens the door, not in the best of humour. He's not a morning person.

The house, two cottages knocked into one, on a smart, steep, terraced street just 50 yards from the Hatton family home, carries the name of the King's hit record. Ricky reckons that's exactly what the place feels like when he's on the wagon, consumed by training and sticking to a diet containing more boring greens than a warren of hungry rabbits could handle.

Ricky throws his overnight bag into the boot of Speaky's silver Merc and they make the 12 mile journey to Manchester Airport in time to catch an 11am flight to Bristol.

Thistle Hotel, Bristol......

7pm......

Ricky's guest of honour at Steve Phillips's testimonial dinner but is relieved to learn it's not black tie. He opts for black pin-stripe suit and open necked black shirt, and makes his way downstairs to the first floor function room.

It's a typical refurbished, Victorian, city centre hotel, apparently 'perfectly situated for exploring the delights of the historic harbour'. It's a venue tonight's organiser Jane Couch knows well. She's boxed on, and promoted fight-nights in the very room now packed with dinner-dance punters.

Round tables are squeezed into the big, high-ceilinged room. There's around 400 here: a mixed bag of men and women, young and old, all turned out in their finest.

8pm......

The top table is elevated across a stage. The 'names' take their seats in the centre. Ricky's next to Gazza, with Jimmy White and Phil Taylor on the other side. Steve Phillips, in whose name they are

here, has been moved out onto the flanks. Well it is often said that goalkeepers secretly want to play outfield.

Other dignitaries include former British and Commonwealth welterweight champion Gary Jacobs, and Mike Tyson's old sparring partner 'Big' Joe Egan. The former Irish heavyweight champ was famously described by Iron Mike as 'the baddest white man on the planet' and the only man he never managed to knock down in training.

The assembled tuck into their meat and three veg – Ricky of course swerving anything on the plate that's not on Kerry's list. The wine and beer are flowing freely throughout the room as the guest speaker reaches for a tempting jug of tap water.

9.15pm......

Gazza – wearing a grey suit with a black shirt undone practically to the belly button – is taking the piss out of Ricky's suit. Most of what he says in rapid-fire Geordie is impossible to follow, but the subject of his abuse is clearly enjoying the banter.

9.27pm......

Meal over, the MC rattles through various messages and thank yous before whipping the now reasonably-greased audience into a whooping frenzy with the announcement of the guest speaker......"the undisputed light-welterweight champion of the world – Ricky 'Hitman' Haaaatttooooonn!"

Ricky stands up, huge grin on his face. He always gets a buzz when he's reminded of just what he's achieved in boxing.

"I have to say, I was quite nervous before I stood up to speak to you all tonight," he says grasping the microphone in his right-hand and holding it close to his mouth. Left hand in left pocket.

"It's always a bit daunting speaking before a large crowd," he begins in a strong, confident voice. "Then I realised what type of people I was dealing with – my kind of people. A load of f****** piss-artists!"

The whole room cheers. You can see a surprised look on many smiling faces. They probably didn't know what to expect. Nice guy that he is, this is no shrinking violet, and he's off.

"I'd like to thank the lovely Jane Couch. It's unbelievable, I've known Jane for so many years

(Pic. Paul Speak)

now and it's funny...........I've never seen her box!"

Jane's in stitches but only a third of the room have understood the gag.

Ricky gives them a jolt, "Wake up – you didn't get that did you?"

He's sticking with Jane for now though and moves seamlessly on to the subject of women boxing.

"I think it's bad when you see women knocking shit out of each other. It's bad enough when you see men knocking lumps out of each other. But I have come around to thinking they are good at what they do and they work just as hard as the men so they deserve respect.

"You know, women we love you, but you are hard work at times. Imagine being a boxing trainer, training a woman? Imagine going to the weigh-in with your fighter?

"Imagine the weigh-in? 'I don't weigh that! I've been on a f****** green week!'"

This one hits the spot straight away and the room roars its approval.

When the applause dies down the Hitman-turned-Showman moves on to another of his favourite targets – Ray Hatton.

"If my father was here now you'd think how the hell has he produced a world champion? He's about four foot nine. He makes Frank Maloney look like f****** Gulliver! He could be a bouncer at Mothercare!

"I apologise, but I don't like midgets. I had a

girlfriend who left me for a midget once. I never thought anyone would stoop that low!"

Glasses and cutlery are being banged on tables now as the well-to-do sport fans of Bristol show their approval amid the clapping, cheering and shouting. As ever, more than a few give it the 'go on Ricky' line.

With everyone well warmed up now, it's time for a bit of proper boxing talk. Ricky speaks a little about his amateur days, turning pro, and then the story of his first big test.

"I've always set myself goals, and the first goal I wanted to achieve was to become British champion. Nowadays you've got so many titles it's a bit of a joke to be honest.

"In one sense it's good for the boxers because they've got more opportunities because there are more belts. But it's not good for the boxing public because you never find out who the best boxer is.

"But I always wanted to fight for the British title and the coveted Lonsdale belt. It's the best belt in boxing bar none and I got a chance to fight for the British title against a fella called Jonathan Thaxton.

"Bearing in mind I had a cut problem early in my career, the bell went for the first round and I'm sure the draft f****** did it, because next minute my head's bursting blood. It wasn't even a good punch.

"I thought, 'Jesus! Jonathan Thaxton, as tough as they come, never been knocked out, eleven rounds to go. I've blown it, I've lost my chance!'

"I sat down on my stool and my cuts man, Mick Williamson, the best cuts man in the job – he's got me out of so much shit – he said to me, 'Ricky what are you feeling sorry about?' I said, 'I've got eleven rounds to go I'm never gonna make it.'

"He said, 'look you've been cut before haven't you?' I said, 'yeah'. He said, 'well you knew you'd get cut again didn't you?' I said, 'yeah'. He said, 'well what you f****** whinging about you little shit – get on with it'."

More laughter followed by applause.

"We ended up going the full 12 rounds and it was a right bloodbath. Thaxton ended up with three cuts and I had this one cut above my eye. It needed 28 stitches and plastic surgery, but it was my first achievement winning that Lonsdale belt."

Ricky pauses to take the applause.

"Jonathan Thaxton was one of the nice guys of boxing. There are so many tossers about in boxing these days, but he's one of the nice guys.

"After the fight we went into the medical room at the Wembley Conference Centre. Thaxton's lying on one bed and I'm lying on the other bed. He's

Gazza was an entertainer, one of the most gifted footballers we've had.

It's nice to see that with the rough ride he's had, he's coming through the other end and looking better for it.

being stitched up and I'm being stitched up over my left eye.

"Then Jon says' 'I tell you what Ricky that was a great fight'. I said, 'it was Jon yeah, I thoroughly enjoyed it!'

"He said, 'that might get fight of the year Ricky?' I said, 'it might do Jon yeah!'

"He said, 'we'll have to do it again Ricky'. I said, 'Jon…….f*** off!'"

Again, the punters make their appreciation known.

Hardly pausing for breath, Ricky rattles on. The crowd are lapping up the tales of past fights with the odd bawdy gag thrown in for good measure.

During one of his anecdotes, a bloke at the back of the room, no doubt fortified by drink, decides a bit of heckling is in order. Rick looks in his direction and smiles menacingly, "if you spend any more time in my hair…….you'll go out without yours!" Arguably the biggest cheer of the night follows.

It's now 49 minutes since Ricky was introduced to the diners. He's still going strong and enjoying himself, but realises time is pressing and wraps up the night. He thanks them all sincerely as they give him a standing ovation.

After Paul Speak has conducted a memorabilia auction of signed photos of the likes of Muhammad Ali, Kostya Tszyu and Pele, the guests besiege the top table looking for their own autographs and photos.

At a testimonial dinner in Bristol, for a local hero footballer, in the presence of Gazza, it's a little Mancunian boxer that's being mobbed.

11.15pm……

After half an hour of posing for snaps and scribbling his best wishes to Aunt Bettie, or whoever, on a now-treasured menu, Ricky is whisked to a room in the wings for a quiet drink with selected VIPs.

It's not the first time he's spoken at a function in Bristol, but he admits to getting a buzz from an 'away' crowd.

"It seems that everywhere I go I do get recognised, but it is very strange. I never think of myself as anything special so when people come and make a fuss in somewhere like Bristol it just makes me think I must be doing something right. It never ceases to amaze me though.

"There were a few ladies in the crowd tonight and I was effin' and jeffin' but that's just me. I'm a working class lad so I'll do a working class speech. A posh audience may not take to it at first, but I think normally by the end of it they realise I'm just a genuine guy. I think in boxing, where there's a lot of bullshit spoken nowadays, people find that refreshing."

Ricky continues to shake hands and pose for pictures but there's no sign of the other sporting stars except for Phil Taylor who has been taking snaps all evening and is now showing off his handiwork to a queue of people at the far end of the room.

Ricky explains, "Well they weren't booked as acts but what is nice is that they've just come down to see me! To be perfectly honest I find that a massive honour. Paul Gascoigne, Jimmy White, they're my heroes in many ways. It's unbelievable!

"Hopefully we'll raise some good money for him (Steve Phillips). If I was having my testimonial dinner I'd hope these kind of people would show me the same kind of respect."

Anybody that has seen Ricky perform his 'act' will have witnessed a man completely at ease in the spotlight.

"There's nothing I like more than standing up on a stage entertaining a crowd and seeing people laugh," he says. "It's normally something you'd do when you retire but I'm still active.

"I'm a boxing fan and I'd have jumped at the chance to go and see the likes of Roberto Duran, Barry McGuigan and Nigel Benn, but normally you'd only get to see them do this when they retire.

"It is very hard to stand up in front of a massive audience and give a speech, but I don't have a set routine. I don't even look at my notes, I just wing it and sometimes I forget how long I've been up there.

"I could be up there for an hour then I'll think, 'shit, I've been on too long now'."

Jane Couch earlier described Ricky as having more than a touch of the young Bernard Manning about him. When Ricky hears this, he stares in mock horror, "What's she trying to say - that I'm a fat bastard?

"Jane's a real genuine person, the type of person I like. I don't like people who blow smoke up your arse. I've known Jane about seven years and I like to think people aren't being my mates for who I am."

There are similarities between public speaking and boxing. The fighter or speaker is under the lights, on their own, a crowd demanding to be entertained, often wanting them to fail. They're both brutal pastimes.

Ricky thinks about this for a second: "Well whatever you do in life you don't want to make a dick of yourself. Whether you're talking or fighting you want to make a good impression.

"When people come up and say you're not just a good fighter but you're also a nice kid, that's priceless. When I retire I'll still want to come to nights like this."

Midnight......

The 'special' guests have now moved from the first VIP room to the second ultra VIP room in a club beneath the hotel. Once down winding stairs there's a small bar area ahead with dark cove rooms shooting off in various directions.

Ricky's still pressing the flesh with an easy charm; drunk blokes telling him, "you're great you Ricky. I f****** love you!"; the cheekier ones with the not-so original, 'I could have you' patter. But it's well intentioned and the big grin is never far from the Hitman's face.

It's the kind of night Ricky would enjoy an awful lot more if he wasn't in the monastery.

Jane Couch flits past, in a figure-hugging little black number that shows off her tattoos and muscular frame. She's still organising everyone and checking everything's okay. The paying customers are nodding and telling her what a great night it is. Who's going to tell her any different?

In Jane, Ricky has a fan for life. "Hatton's just quality as a speaker and I knew he wouldn't let me down," she says in a strong, deep, Lancashire accent not chipped away from years living in Bristol.

"Once you know Ricky Hatton, and everyone knows what a great speaker he is, you can then ring Gazza, you can ring Phil Taylor coz it gives you credibility.

"If Ricky hadn't been here tonight, none of the others would have turned up. He's just a quality, quality bloke. He's so down to earth.

"I look after people when I get them here. I don't treat them like shit. I can always ask them to come back. I never take the piss out of anyone.

"I've known Ricky a long, long time, you know just through the boxing world. We're from the same part of the world and we both know where we're coming from. I respect him and he respects me. He's just a great mate."

So she obviously doesn't mind him taking the

Ricky wakes up to find his old 'mates' Gazza, Phil Taylor and Gary Jacobs have broken into his room. (Pic. Paul Speak)

piss out of women boxers then?

"Well he will do won't he? He was f****** funny though, even I laughed! He was havin' a laugh. If he wants to take the piss out me, he can because he's me pal.

"If he wasn't Ricky Hatton, he wouldn't get away with it. He knows what I can do. Some women boxers aren't the best in the world, but he knows I'm good."

There was a time in the 1990s when the 'Fleetwood Assassin' was something of a household name. If you ask anyone on the high street today to name a female British boxer, if you get an answer at all, it will be Jane Couch. But she's turned her back on the world of celebrity to concentrate on the sport she loves.

"I used to do all the shows, like *Michael Barrymore*, and people got to know me for doing those shows and not for my fighting. So I stopped it. I don't do interviews anymore. I'm doing an interview for this book because of Ricky, because

he's done me a favour.

"I don't want to be famous for being on *Barrymore* or *Frank Skinner*. I'm a fighter, and a good fighter. As long as the boxing people know about me that's all I care about. I don't care about the public.

"I get calls to do shows every day but I don't do it anymore. It was a mistake. I've got the respect of the boxing world now. If I went on shows again I wouldn't have it. You're just a slag when you box for them, and I'm one hundred percent a fighter. I don't want to be known as a celebrity.

"I've boxed on the same bill as Mike Tyson, Naseem Hamed, Lennox Lewis, Roy Jones Jnr and a million other undercards in America and that suits me. I'm not gonna go on f****** *Paul O'Grady* and *Richard and Judy*. I've done all that."

Jane, it's fair to say, is passionate about boxing. A 'disrespectful' comment could lead to dire consequences for a cheeky punter.

"Listen! I've been boxing for 14 years and I

haven't made a penny. The most I ever got paid for a world title fight was seven thousand dollars.

"The media made it a circus. My first fight in London was pathetic. There were photographers from Cosmopolitan. They should have been boxing people."

Back on the subject of her best boxing mate, and the mood lightens again.

"Everything about Ricky is champion," she says. "He's absolute class. He's so down to earth.

"In the ring, Ricky is one of the most exciting fighters in the world. His idol was Roberto Duran. He's like Roberto Duran. He goes forward and he's the best body puncher ever to come out of this country.

"Everyone goes on about Calzaghe but Ricky Hatton is the best British fighter we've got and we should cherish him. That's the trouble with this country, we don't do that enough with our fighters.

"Nobody gave him a chance against Kostya Tszyu and he destroyed him."

Jane is in training for a bout in Birmingham on 6 May and is then heading out to America for a world title fight in July. As a light-welterweight herself, she's confident Ricky will make the step up to welterweight without any problems.

"I boxed on the undercard of Callazo back in 1999 and he is a good fighter, but Ricky will beat him. I've no doubt about that. Ricky will destroy him because he [Collazo] is not the strongest welterweight in the world. He's a very good fighter but Ricky will be too strong. Not killing himself to make the weight, people might see the best of Ricky Hatton.

"Listen, that kid is class. Everyone's waiting for him to get beat because that's what British people do. But I don't think he ever will."

Jane makes a move as there's more organising to be done. She stops for a chat with Steve Phillips.

With everyone making a fuss of Ricky it's easy to forget it's actually Steve's testimonial night – a reward for ten years' service at Ashton Gate. But even he knows he's not the star of his own show.

"The people of Bristol haven't come to see me tonight," he smiles. "You could have charged fifty to a hundred pound for people to come and see Ricky on his own, let alone with Gazza, Phil Taylor, Jimmy White etc. As long as people go home happy, that's all that counts.

"I thought he [Ricky] was very funny. He used a lot of humour to make some serious points about his own career, but he used up all the time! I didn't even get chance to get on the microphone! He was fantastic!"

1.10am......

Ricky's disappeared, but the party is in full flow.

Sunday, 2 April......

9.20am......

Ricky wakes up to find his old 'mates' Gazza, Phil Taylor and Gary Jacobs have broken into his room and decided to autograph his shoes with a gold marker pen.

He partly has himself to blame after telling Gazza last night that he was due to head straight from Bristol to Yorkshire TV today to film *Bullseye*. He doesn't have a spare pair of shoes.

Midday......

After returning to the hotel, after a quick shopping spree in the city centre to buy some new footwear, Ricky meets the car Yorkshire TV have sent down to collect him, and heads north.

"I had to get up extra early to go around a load of shoe shops or I'd have looked a right dickhead! It was quite timid though for Gazza, I got away lucky."

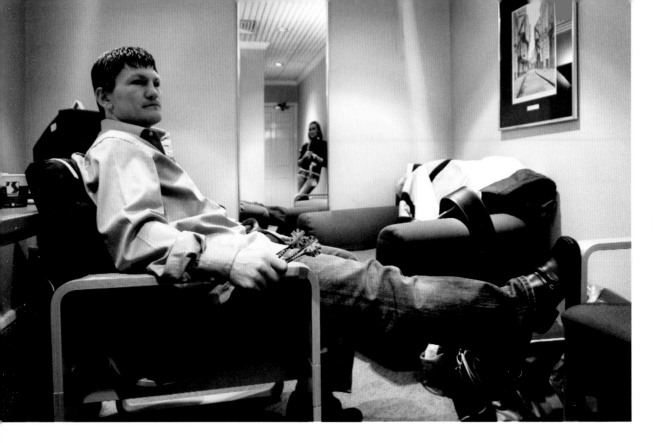

Yorkshire TV, Leeds……

4pm……

Ricky and Speaky arrive in Leeds and are greeted by the show's producer who settles them into their dressing room next to the Green Room.

The celebrity thrower gets changed into a fresh shirt and jeans and, after showing off his friends' handiwork, puts on his new boots. He then heads to the Green Room and meets the three couples who will battle it out to compete for Bully's star prize.

There's a dartboard hanging at the back of the room, so Ricky takes the opportunity to get a bit of practice in, and he's throwing well. The host Dave Spikey (Jim Bowen's replacement) and announcer Tony Green pop in to say hello before everybody heads outside for filming.

Back-to-back episodes are being filmed ahead of the show's return, this time to Challenge TV, later this month. As one set of contestants leaves the set, so the new programme starts.

Excited Bully fans in the studio audience – including Speaky – get ready for filming as Ricky awaits his call in the wings. The format to the programme is just about the same as the 1980s version, but Spikey knows better than to hijack all Jim's cult catchphrases, so there'll be no 'super, smashing, great'. That said, the old standards are still there: 'you can't beat a bit of Bully', 'stay out of the black and into the red' (cue studio audience to finish the immortal line) 'there's nothing in this game for two in a bed'.

During a brief break in recording while a small technical hitch is sorted, Spikey – a stand-up comedian who came to prominence in Peter Kay's *Phoenix Nights* as Jerry St Clair, the Compere without Compare – puts his quiz cards down and turns to have a bit of banter with the audience.

"You know I've had a terrible day," he says in his broad Bolton accent. "Every morning when I wake up, I go over to the window and open the curtains and everyday there's a German Shepherd having a shit on my lawn… I wouldn't mind but today he even brought his dog!"

You had to be there.

Back to filming, and after some truly dismal dart throwing performances from the contestants, it's Ricky's turn to take the oche. He's reminded by

Dave and Tony that he has to throw nine darts, he gets a pound a point for the contestants' chosen charity which is doubled if he scores 301 or more.

Ricky's introduced as 'a very special guest' and on he walks. He's brought his replica IBF and WBA belts with him so he has a quick chat with Spikey about the belts and the upcoming fight, then it's up to the oche.

"Take yer time Ricky," Tony says in his familiar, reassuring Yorkshire voice.

Ricky fires off his nine darts. He gets close to the treble 20 with just about every dart but doesn't reach the magical 301. He has to make do with 165, but a decent effort.

Back in the wings, Ricky watches on as a father and son team beat the other two couples to make it to the final.

They now have the agonising decision whether or not to keep the toaster or gamble and go for the speedboat (or whatever prize there might be behind the curtain). You could cut the tension in the studio with a knife as Dave tells them they have the time until the board has revolved to make a decision.......they look at each other......they nod........ "we're gonna gamble Dave!" The crowd is prompted to roar approval.

Between them they have to get 101 or more with the 'non-dart player' throwing first. As neither of them appear to have seen a dart board before it's no shock when they fail miserably. Couldn't hit a cow's arse with a shovel.

With the same perverse glee that Jim Bowen so enjoyed, Dave says, "Now look what you could have won!"

Disappointingly it's not a speedboat that's wheeled out from behind the curtain by the models, but instead two shiny scooters that they won't be going home on.

The losing couple and the other contestants hide their disappointment well when they all pile into Ricky's dressing room after the recording, looking for autographs and photos. The woman from Essex says meeting the Hitman is the highlight of her day. Ricky thanks her very much.

Dave and Tony have pictures taken with Ricky in the studio wings amid lights, cables and TV monitors. Tony in particular is a big Hatton fan and is telling him all about his love of boxing and how he watches all his fights.

They say their goodbyes and Team Hatton leaves the building, jumps into a people carrier and heads back over the Pennines.

"I don't think I could change my profession to darts, although I could probably match the darts players in the drinking department!"

Tony Green (left) and Dave Spikey (right) with Ricky and Bully (Pic. Paul Speak)

Musical Youth

Monday, 3 April......

1.20pm......

A fairly hectic, but physically inactive, weekend so Ricky's back in the gym at the normal time throwing himself into training like a man possessed.

He's been on the bags, pads and bar for the past 45 minutes and is showing no sign of letting up the pace.

As usual Kerry appears at the gym to take his lunch break. The first sight that greets him is Ricky going bananas, pounding the heavy bag like a Duracel boxing bunny. He's hitting the bag so hard he has it swinging all over the place. The steel girder that runs across the ceiling, taking the weight of the bag, is rattling and bouncing and making a right racket.

A smiling Kerry stands ten feet away, hands on hips and asks no-one in particular, loud enough so Ricky can hear, "Who's upset him today?"

Ricky takes a break and decides it's time for some music. He makes his way into the office and puts Smooth FM on the gym stereo. To the funky lurve strains of Barry White, he goes back to banging the bag – singing along in between shots.

"You're my first! Nnaaargh, nnaaargh. My last! Nnaaargh, naaargh. My everything!"

The choice of radio station is interesting, but the two Matthews don't seem too pleased. Ricky's the top dog in this gym though, it's his say, and he likes a bit of love in the afternoon.

"You've got to be in a pecking order," he states. "I remember when I was 18 or 19 I was down the pecking order to lads like Carl Thompson, Ensley Bingham and Steve Foster Senior. You have to work your way up the ladder.

"It's nice that I have the choice of radio station now. Generally I pick the music just to piss the rest of them off!

"When the training gets a little more intense I'll up the music. I'll start banging Oasis on and the Red Hot Chillies. I like rock music and it tends to get me going.

"But really, my favourite music is the golden oldies. So while the training isn't intense, to the disgust of the other boxers in the gym, I put on Smooth FM and listen to the golden oldies."

Matthew Hatton shouts over, "I like Smooth FM, but not to train to! I like music that gets you going. It drives me mad sometimes.

"When his back's turned we'll change over so it can get a bit daft sometimes."

It's Matthew Macklin's turn now. He says he's waiting for the day he's number one fighter in the gym, "Then it'll be, Smooth FM?........f*** off!"

1.35pm......

Another familiar sight in the gym makes his noisy entrance. Ted Peate was Ricky's first amateur trainer and mentor, the man who witnessed the Hitman's first boxing steps. To this day, Ted is still a boxing father figure to Ricky.

A short man in his late 60s with thinning white hair and now carrying just a few extra pounds around the waist, Ted's making his way through the gym when Ricky spots him and kicks off the banter.

"Have you lost weight Ted?" he asks very insincerely. "F****** fallin' off me," Ted fires back without breaking step. Today he's arrived at the gym on a mission to get hold of some free boxing gear for the kids at his gym in Hyde. He's not shy.

He wanders around the gym like everyone's favourite uncle at a party, cracking jokes and having a go at all the lads. After he's finished telling everybody what kit he'd like, he departs to the canteen for a cup of tea.

Ted picks up the story of the early days, "Ricky first came into my gym when he was ten, so I said to him, 'just have a go on that bag son' and I looked over and he was getting stuck into the bag. I said, 'bloody hell he'll make one'.

"So I went over to him, I put on the pads and even though he was only ten I could feel the shots.

"He'd done a bit of kick-boxing so maybe that's why he was keeping his feet on the floor when he hit, 'cos kids normally lift their feet when they hit.

"Anyway, I took Ricky for his first fight in

Liverpool. The kid he was going to fight had had three fights and won three. Normally you wouldn't take that for a kid having his first fight. But I thought I'll have that, I fancy this kid.

"Anyway Ricky tore him to pieces, and the fella giving the prizes out at the end was an Everton and former City player. The beauty for Ricky wasn't winning the fight, but getting his picture taken with a City player."

Ted can't remember the name of the footballer. A few yards away, Ricky is working on the step machine. "Mark Ward" he shouts over.

"Then there was the time I took him to a tournament in Denmark," Ted continues without drawing breath. "When we got off the plane I asked Ricky if he had his passport. He said 'no'. I asked what he'd done with it; he said he'd left it on the plane. I asked him why he'd done that and he said 'well I'll need it for going home!'"

What about the Ricky we see today. Has all the success, fame and money corrupted the little working class kid he's known for 17 years?

"Ricky's never ever changed. He's the same now as when he was ten," he says.

"I've had tickets for every fight wherever he's had a fight. I've never even asked for them, but he always comes round to the house and drops off a couple of tickets every time.

"I could tell him now that I had a boxing show tomorrow and, even if he was going to America the day after, he'd turn up at the show. When he turns up all the kids are around him like a fly-trap. He walks in and the gym stops.

"If you walk around Hyde with him, everyone wants to talk to him and he doesn't mind. You get pissed off because you have to stop four or five times. Even if you're having a cup of tea in the café, people want to talk to him, but he never minds."

As Ted sips his tea, Ricky, who's now showered and changed, joins him. But Ted doesn't mind. The old master and student continue their banter from before.

Ricky orders a coffee and the conversation about the old days carries on. He may have world titles and money now, but memories from his amateur days don't fade.

"You know what?" Ricky says while stirring his recently arrived coffee. "One of the proudest moments of my career was when I represented my country. The first time I put the England vest on, coming out to the national anthem. That was one of my best moments.

"There was one night though when it went pear-shaped. I remember the first time I ever boxed for England. I was 17 years of age boxing for Young England in Germany.

"I boxed a kid called Jurgen Braemer. He was about six foot tall and very skinny. I looked at him and thought, 'this is perfect for me; he's got loads of ribs to aim at. I'll hit him with a few body shots'.

"Bell rang for the first round so I think come on.......Bang!......I'm flat on my arse!

"This German hit me and my head bounced off the floor. Hundreds of ring lights were shining down on the canvas. The canvas was royal blue. It just so happens, that at this time, the bed sheet on my bed was also royal blue.

"All I could see were the lights shining down, and I swear to God, I thought it was the sun shining through my bedroom, it was morning and I had to go running!

"Anyway, I looked up and this German's going 'eins, zwei, drei' – then I looked at the corner and they've got their heads in their hands. I thought, 'Jesus, I've got a f****** fight here!'

"He hit me a few shots. He hit me with a right, with a left. I was like an MFI wardrobe, I was all over the shop.

"Next minute my corner's thrown the towel in. It was the first time I'd ever been stopped in my life.

"Six weeks later I boxed the same guy again in a multi-nation tournament in Sardinia. So I thought, right I'll have him this time. That's how stupid I was!

"Not only did he knock me out the first time – he beat me again on points. So not only was he the only person to knock me out, he beat me twice!

"Thank f*** the German bastard's retired!"

"I've got a five-year-old lad now and he's got football boots and he kicks a ball about. There are no gloves in sight in his bedroom put it that way."

The chat continues with Ted joking that he's still living off the fact that he's the man who discovered Ricky Hatton. Despite all the cracks and piss-taking, he obviously could not be prouder of his association with the champ.

He admits to being disappointed when Ricky went professional at 18 because he wanted him to win an Olympic or Commonwealth medal. But with hindsight, agrees it was the smartest move he could have made.

Ricky did win a bronze medal at the 1996 World Amateur Championships, but it's not a prize he cherishes.

"I threw the medal in a draw and haven't looked at it since," he says with a touch of bitterness still.

"In amateur boxing people always say, 'I was robbed', but I knocked lumps out of him and I didn't get the decision. It was that bad a decision the world governing body did an inquiry into the judging and they found that the Russian team had paid off judges. Even so it didn't help me, I still only had a bronze medal, but it did help me feel a little bit better about myself."

In between rare sips of his tea, it's tale after tale. Ted, a man who lives for boxing, shakes his head sadly as he speaks of his five children.

"All daughters!......Five bleedin' daughters!" He's off again.

"One of them lives in Australia, so when Ricky boxed Kostya Tszyu and won, I sent two of my granddaughters Ricky Hatton t-shirts. On the Monday they went to school in the t-shirts and the teacher kicked them out! He said, 'you're not wearing them in school'. Anyway, as they were leaving for home they bumped into the headmaster who asked them why they were out of class.

"They explained that Mr so-and-so had kicked them out because of the t-shirts. The Headmaster then told them to go back to class. He told them to tell the teacher that he too was a Mancunian, and that they can wear their t-shirts and that's that. So they went back to class pleased as punch.

"The kids reckon the teacher fell out with them, but now they get on dead well with the headmaster!"

The 'Hitman' Hatton listens to the 'Boastful' Christian.

Tuesday, 4 April......

BBC, Oxford Road, Manchester

9am......

Ricky's been invited on to Terry Christian's radio show as a special guest to coincide with the renaming of GMR (Greater Manchester Radio) to Radio Manchester.

Paul Speak's been up early. He left his Radcliffe home at 7am, drove to Ricky's house in Hyde, got a grumpy Hitman out of bed and headed into town.

They arrive on time and are whisked straight into the 'live' studio during a break. Terry greets everyone, Ricky then takes his seat, puts on his headphones and the red studio 'on-air' light comes back on. Formalities out of the way, they get down to the nitty gritty.

TC: So the next fight's in America, are you getting good coverage in the States?

RH: Very good coverage. HBO have just signed a

three-fight deal with me, which is rare for a British fighter. I've been over there a few times recently. Whenever I've finished my fight and there's a big fight on in Vegas or Madison Square Garden, I go over for a bit of a holiday and a celebration.

It's weird now since the Kostya Tszyu fight, Americans recognise me in the street.

TC: Do you get the red carpet treatment?

RH: Yeah a little bit. You might expect it walking through Deansgate but certainly not walking down Times Square. Hopefully they'll be working on a blue carpet for next time I'm there!

TC: A lot of people think boxers just turn up and get loads of money. They don't know about the months of training, no beer, no chocolate.

RH: Well that's about the gist of it. I train for 12 weeks before every fight. Dieting, running, sparring and if that isn't hard enough you've got the fight after that. Believe you me it hurts when you get punched!

During a music break, Terry and Ricky talk football. Christian's as big a United fan as Ricky is City so there are a few jibes flying from both sides. The presenter's telling his guest about some of the nutters from Hyde who used to follow United in the '80s.

It was all before Ricky's time of course, but the youthful Christian reveals he's now 43. He's looking good on it – "never worked for a livin' though have I?" he says in his best nasal whine.

After Westlife, or whoever it was, have finished squealing their merry tune, it's back to the chat.

TC: What about your mum, she can't like you fighting?

RH: Well I've been doing it since I was ten years of age so I think they've got used to it, but it can't be nice for them. I know when my brother Matthew boxes I feel physically sick, my nerves just go to pieces.

I think it's just due to the fact that when you're in the ring you can do something about it but when your brother's in the ring getting punched it's hard to see.

I've got a five-year-old lad now and he's got football boots and he kicks a ball about. There are no gloves in sight in his bedroom put it that way.

TC: Have you taken him to City?

RH: Yes - you have to set young kids on the right road! He could say 'City' before he could say 'dad!' I take him to the match, in the box, and he sings for about five minutes then gets his toys out.

His mum's side of the family are all United fans,

and when my back's turned our Matthew will be telling him to say 'Man United', so he'll make his own mind up.

9.50am......

Interview over, goodbyes all round. Christian goes back to his hotseat, while Ricky leaves the studio to head for a hotseat of his own. He's going back to school.

Alder Community High School, Gee Cross, Hyde......

10.30am......

For his second engagement of the day, Ricky's agreed to talk to kids at his old school. Hattersley High has now changed its name to Alder Community High, and moved to a new site down the road, but many of the teachers who taught him remain.

The pupils have been told they have a special guest for their Personal and Social Health Education lesson, but don't know who it is.

There are posters all around the room warning of society's various dangers from sexually transmitted diseases to alcohol and drugs. It's terrifying stuff.

The youngsters spill into class and look impressed when they spot a local TV crew and a few other dodgy looking press types all stood at the back of the room. They're a bit excited now.

Ricky's waiting in a book cupboard with his IBF belt over one shoulder and the WBA version slung over the other. When the kids are settled, he makes his not-so dramatic entrance and takes his seat in

"After I finish boxing I might be a trainer. I want to stay in sport and use the knowledge I've learnt to teach others, whatever their sport."

front of them.

Some of the class, particularly the girls, are visibly underwhelmed. Boxing might not be their thing. What did they expect? David Beckham? Maybe it's because Ricky, as he always says, is simply one of them. They're probably used to seeing him around. He only lives a few hundred yards away and he passes the school every day on his run.

The class teacher, Paula Parker, introduces the Hitman and he gives them a little talk about his own experiences at school.

"I wasn't much of a troublemaker," he starts "but I could have done more with my schoolwork. I wouldn't have had anything to fall back on if my boxing hadn't worked out.

"When you're 16 years of age and you leave school after being a bit of a ratbag and not doing your school work, it's going to set you back for the rest of your life.

"I don't know what I'd be doing if I hadn't made it as a boxer. I'd be in a whole lot of trouble 'cos it's a difficult world when you leave school."

He goes on to tell them that sport and academic work should go hand in hand, how if your brain's ticking over, your sport will benefit.

"Look at Teddy Sheringham," he offers as an example, "he's still playing in the Premiership at 40 because of his brain.

"A lot of people think boxing is all about the strongest man or the toughest man getting in a ring and winning. It's not like that at my level.

"When you're fighting 12 rounds your tactics might change three, four or five times during the fight. So if you haven't got the type of brain that can change tactics like that in a fight then you're gonna be in trouble. You have to be a bit clever.

"There's so much more to boxing: there's the diet, looking after your body and I'd like to think that after I finish boxing I might be a trainer. I want to stay in sport and use the knowledge I've learnt to teach others, whatever their sport."

The pupils have listened quietly to Ricky's wise words. He's as comfortable sitting chatting to kids as he is dealing with drunken hecklers at a sportsman's dinner.

One of the lads paying particular attention is 14 year old Danny Benson. He boxes at Ted Peate's gym and recently won the Golden Gloves ABA 75kg division.

"I want to be a pro like Ricky," Danny says while his idol poses for photos with his classmates after the talk.

"I aim to win the ABAs then go pro at 19 or 20. I want to go to the Olympics first though in 2012.

"Ricky comes down the gym a lot and he's an inspiration. Ted says he hasn't changed. He says he's just like he was when he was a kid even though he's won a world title.

"He gives advice when he's down the gym. He'll have you on the pads sometimes and he'll be telling you how to throw your punches and that."

Mr Owen, Ricky's former PE teacher grabs a word with his old star pupil. He shows off a note Ray Hatton had written asking for Ricky to be excused from sport that day as he'd pulled a muscle.

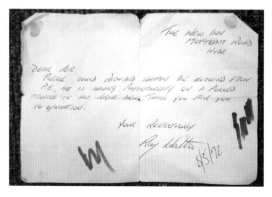

Don't Believe the Hype

Wednesday, 5 April......

Betta Bodies Gym Canteen......

3pm......

Another 'hard' day's training is at an end. Billy strapped on the body-belt for the first time in this particular camp. Ricky beat him up for four rounds.

"As you can see I'm jumping the bar, and I've just started on the belt which is a big part of the training. Over the next week or two I'll start sparring. The training gets harder and harder.

"Billy's ecstatic with the way things are going with my training," he adds. "I'm more powerful and faster. Billy actually said I've never felt so sharp or good with six weeks to go till the fight.

"Everything's right with my diet and my training's good. In fact I'm lifting heavier weights than I've ever lifted."

Yesterday Ricky had been tearing all over the place before training had even begun. A straightforward session today with no distractions.

"It'll calm down now," he says "I think I've got two more functions and then I'll knock it on the head.

"Don't get me wrong, the training's not easy at the moment, but as it's a little bit more comfortable at the minute, it's nice to get away and have a little bit of an unwind. But the training gets more intense by the week now so functions become less and less."

Ricky finishes his day at the gym by signing dozens of pictures of himself that Speaky, who does a nice line in memorabilia, is putting in front of him.

Billy walks past, says "see ya" to all there and heads for the stairs.

What does he think of Ricky's extra-curricular activities? Isn't it a distraction working the after-dinner circuit during training?

Billy thinks for a few seconds then says, "I actually like him doing it. He likes to go up on stage and he likes to talk. He's a ham! He enjoys it and it helps him relax so it does him good, know what I mean?

"I've heard he's good at the speaking stuff, but I really don't like it when it's too close to a fight. It's nearly coming to an end now. He'll have to just wait because when it gets close to a fight, nothing can interfere with training. Nothing at all.

"It pisses me off if he gets dates close to a fight and we're coming to that soon."

Thursday, 6 April......

Ricky and his dad Ray are finalising plans for a trip out to Boston on Saturday morning to promote the Collazo fight.

Fight Academy's American partners Banner Promotions have organised a press conference. It'll be the first time Ricky's been Stateside since the US boxing writers voted him their fighter of the year. It's the first time a Briton has won the honour.

It'll also be the first time Ricky meets Luis Collazo face-to-face, but he's not up for any nonsense.

"All the eyeballing lark," he says with a shrug, "I've been there and seen it all before. If someone tries to eyeball me I don't bat an eyelid.

"At this level, I wouldn't even attempt it. You're

fighting world champions or former world champions so it's a load of bollocks really. Fight fans like to see it, it gets their juices flowing but I don't go in for it.

"Some fighters do it, but everyone's different. You can get the arrogance of Eubank or Naseem Hamed, you know - 'I'm gonna knock you out' and all that. Maybe I'm a refreshing alternative, I don't know. I don't do the trash-talk."

The 'not bovvered' attitude hasn't always been the case. Ricky has been wound up in the past.

"Just once, with Eamonn Magee, but it was inexperience. He was bad-mouthing me and I didn't particularly rate him.

"I thought, 'you've got a nerve saying all these things about me'. I thought he was way out of his depth. I took him lightly and even though I beat him comfortably, I learned a valuable lesson. Nowadays I just laugh it off."

What had he been saying?

"Oh, just how he was gonna knock me out, how he'd never been put down and never been stopped. The usual shit."

And he put you down in that fight.

"He did yeah and it taught me a valuable lesson. Don't listen!"

Ricky with number one fan James Bowes

Friday, 7 April......

The Cottage Pub, Denton......

7.30pm......

The pub is packed. It's ticket-only tonight and the two doormen and one doorwoman aren't playing games. If you haven't got a ticket or your name's not on the list............you're not coming in.

The DJ's been spinning some cheesy tunes and at the back of the pub there are framed photos of Ricky along with all sorts of sporting memorabilia. Later, all the items will be auctioned off to raise funds to send the Hitman's number one fan to Boston.

Seventeen year-old James Bowes who suffered from hydrocephalus and has epilepsy tries to get to every Ricky Hatton fight. He has often led the way into the ring holding up one of his idol's belts, and is one of the special few allowed into the ring post-fight to celebrate victory.

James arrives with Paul Speak who's been to his home in Hattersley to pick him up.

8.00pm……

Ricky is, of course, guest of honour tonight. He's happy to come along and show support even though he intends to pay for James to travel to Boston in any case. He thinks of James as one of the family, but he also understands the locals want to do their bit for the kid, and doesn't want to make a big deal out of it.

He turns up, showered and changed, after his evening run. It takes an age for him to make his way to the back of the pub as everyone wants a shake of his hand as dozens of mobile phone cameras capture the moment.

Big Joe Egan's also here to lend a hand. Incidentally, ticketless Joe walked into the pub unchallenged. How strange?

The night's a big success.

"It's absolutely fantastic," is Ricky's assessment. "It's only a little pub, a local pub, and it's nice to see people like this.

"Sometimes I go to these sportsman's dinners and there'll be people there who've got their own companies and they don't give 30 bob.

"You go to a little pub where people don't have much money and items [in the auction] are going for 350 or 400 quid. It's outstanding and I'm surprised about the turnout as well. It's about six-deep outside, with people looking in the window.

"It just shows you how much people think of me, but also of little James as well.

"There are people from the council estates of Hyde, Hattersley and Denton, people who may only have 50 pound in their pockets on a night out and they are giving that to James. It's nice to see."

The baddest white man on the planet – Big Joe Egan (front).

Saturday, 8 April......

Five weeks to fight-night......

While Ray and Ricky Hatton leave for their promotional visit to Boston, there's disappointing news for Matthew Macklin.

Jamie Moore has pulled out of their 5 May British light-middleweight clash with a recurrence of an old shoulder injury.

* IBF welterweight champion Floyd Mayweather Junior beats Zab Judah on a unanimous points decision for the vacant IBO welterweight title in the Thomas and Mack center in Las Vegas.

Tuesday, 11 April......

Ray and Ricky arrive home from Boston.

Wednesday, 12 April......

6.30pm......

Ricky's been through a tough session back in the gym today with Billy, although he did manage to

improvise with his training and kept ticking over while he was away.

Ricky's house, or Heatbreak Hotel, is smartly furnished. Memorabilia lines the walls of the large living/games room. There's a dartboard, jukebox and even a karaoke machine. A huge flat screen TV dominates one side of the room and a pool table sits proudly in the middle.

Outside, on the edge of the garden, is a yellow Robin Reliant exact replica Delboy Trotter van - such is Ricky's love of *Only Fools and Horses*. Only eight of those vans exist apparently.

Along the side of the house he's bolted on a row of seats he salvaged from City's old Maine Road ground when it was being demolished.

But back to Boston, and it sounds like he was treated well.

"I went to see the Boston Bruins – the ice hockey team, and they got me on the ice to have a puck. They introduced me to the crowd and told them about the title fight.

"Next night, Sunday, they got me on court at the Boston Celtics. I made a dick of myself again, stood between these six foot ten inch basketball players. It made the national papers and you can imagine - me down here, them up there. I looked a right dick!"

After Ricky had finished feeling a dick, he had

the serious business of plugging the fight to contend with.

"It was good from the PR point of view and I saw Collazo for the first time in the flesh. Don King the promoter was there – that was an experience!

"My American promoter Art Pellulo got up and spoke for a quick five minutes, Dennis Hobson likewise. Don King gets up – fifty f****** minutes he was up!

"He was talking about George Bush, Tony Blair, the War of Independence, the Boston Tea Party. I was sitting there thinking – by the time my turn comes to speak I'm not gonna know what to say! Typical Don King. In many ways it was bullshit, but you'd buy a ticket to watch it! Nobody can sell a show like him!

"When he'd finished, one of the American guys turned to us and said, 'Oh Don's not got much to say today, he's normally up for an hour and half!'

"Anyway, I had a bit of a face-off with Collazo, but with five weeks to go there was no snarling or anything like that.

"He looked confident. He said a lot of people had been talking about Ricky and Mayweather and how he was gonna upset the show.

"But I've never looked past anybody. Mayweather is the big fight, but I always look at whoever's standing in my way and it makes me more determined to get past them.

"He's a bit taller than me. I'd seen the tapes of him obviously. He looks a bit of a speed-merchant and looking at his frame, he's two or three inches taller and a slender build.

"I'm a body puncher so I like people to be a couple of inches taller than me. I punch up from the floor with the big legs that I have, so I'm happy with what I've seen.

"He's obviously a class act. When he won the world title he was a late sub. He took the fight at two weeks' notice and to win the world title with two weeks' notice is unbelievable really."

And what did you say at the press conference?

"I just said I was happy to be in Boston and that I'd been taken to heart by fight fans who seem to like my style and personality, and how I hope the American fight fans take me to their hearts.

"I said that Collazo was certainly talking confident, and Don King's certainly confident. But there's one thing about talking – it doesn't help you in the ring.

"But I was complimentary to him and he was complimentary to me. It's nice to have two fighters like that. He was confident, but nice with it, like me. There was no bad-mouthing or anything like that, and that's the way it should be.

"His family came up to me and had their picture taken with me, which was nice really.

"But he was confident; I could tell by the way he stared at me. But he did it all with a bit of class."

What about Don King? What did he say to you?

"He just said he liked my fighting. He spoke to my dad as well and said we do things right as a family – never bad-mouthing anybody. He's just a larger than life character.

"We went for a coffee and he said [Rick attempts a crazed Don King impression] 'Well it's great to see Ricky Hatton over in the States…and not only Ricky Hatton but little Ray Hatton as well! And I spoke to Tony Blair and he's so excited about this…' We were just sat there thinkin'……..f*** off! What's all this shit! But you know, that's him."

"I've never looked past anybody. I always look at whoever's standing in my way and it makes me more determined to get past them."

"If you have to be told to diet, and train and go to bed early, you're not the champion or fighter you think you are. You shouldn't need people harpin' on at you."

No Easter Eggs

Thursday, 13 April……

3.10pm……

Billy's getting ready to leave the gym. What's the latest regarding the Jamie Moore v Matthew Macklin fight?

"Well we've still got the title shot. It's just been put back a bit. It's disappointing.

"Matthew's excited about the fight, I'm excited about the fight, but these things happen in boxing. Nothing can be done about it so we just have to wait.

"At first we thought Jamie was going to give the title up so we'd then fight for the vacant title and defend against Jamie if we won. But I've found out now that that doesn't look like being the case.

"You have to learn to deal with these things when you're a fighter. But he still can't have any Easter eggs."

Billy slings his kit bag over his shoulder. He doesn't appear to be in a chatty mood. Any update on Ricky's progress?

"He's looking fantastic. He's more than on time. I'm well pleased," the Preacher's mood softens. "The weight's flying off him and he's beginning to look like Ricky Hatton again.

"We'll start sparring soon and do the same things we always do. No need to change a winning formula.

"I've just been told of an American sparring partner. A top kid who's sparred with some top names – he's coming in. We've got people from over here coming in as well.

"We want to go to Boston and give them a treat and show them that Ricky's the most exciting fighter in the world."

Good Friday, 14 April……

Ricky officially confirms he's giving up his IBF belt.

In a letter to the organisation, he writes:

It is with the greatest regret that I must surrender my IBF Light-Welterweight Title. Winning the IBF Championship was without doubt the greatest night of my life and to have to give it up outside of the ring is truly a painful experience. Much worse than the punches I had to take to wrestle the title from Kostya!

It has never been my or my team's intention not to defend my title against the IBF's appointed challenger but sadly due to outside influences, legal problems and problems meeting TV schedules, it seems that this is the situation I find myself in.

I have worn my championship with pride and I hope that in winning the unification bout with Carlos Maussa, I have also made the IBF proud of their champion.

I hope that in the near future I will get the opportunity to become an IBF World Champion again and that I will have the chance to defend my title. Like all fighters, we take great risks in the pursuit of our dreams of becoming World Champions and I hope that in the future I will only win and lose titles in the ring.

Once again I would like to thank you all for the time I spent as your champion and look forward to becoming one again soon, although in my heart I will remain your champion!

Ricky 'Hitman' Hatton.

Meanwhile, it's emerged the WBA is yet to sanction the Hatton v Collazo fight.

After failing in his bid to stop Ricky fighting Maussa in November, Souleymane M'baye is putting further obstacles in the way of the 13 May contest.

Saturday, 15 April......

Four weeks to fight-night......

Gee Cross, Hyde......

Ricky's having an easy day at home. It's a good time to reflect on his training camp from his lofty perch in the monastery.

The weekends can be slow for a social animal like the Hitman, but he knows he can't cave in to temptation and sneak out for a cheeky couple of pints.

"If you've any ambition, you take a job seriously don't you?" He says. "If you write a book you don't want people saying it was a load of crap do you? You knuckle down to it.

"Everyone's entitled to a bad fight, but if I have an off performance, it pisses me right off. It makes me so much more focused to succeed.

"It's like taking food out of my son's mouth. It's stopping him having the best things in life.

"I like to enjoy myself when I'm out of training, I like my food and a good drink and a good time. So when I'm back in the gym it's more of a sacrifice for me than it is for most people.

"I'm training every day, running every day, dieting every day. I have to lose two and a half stone for this fight. I want the best for my son Campbell.

"All these things come into your mind in the ring and the red mist descends. That's the way I am.

"If I trained for 12 weeks and then only had two weeks off, then another 12 weeks training. I'd be thinking, 'I've only had a fortnight off.'

"Some people might be alright with that if they don't like to go out, or they don't like a drink or don't have a massive social life.

"If I went straight back into training like that, after about four or five weeks I'd be more likely to go and have a sneaky night out the nearer the fight gets. I'd be thinking, 'I haven't had enough rest and unwind.'

"After a fight I like to have a couple of holidays, take my son away and have a good feed. After 12 weeks of pasta and fish and boiled potatoes and green veg. I mean, I like it but f****** hell!"

By his own admission, the first couple of weeks of training are the worst. He knows he could probably get away with the odd pint or takeaway, but it's a slippery slope he doesn't want to ride.

"It makes it all the sweeter afterwards. When you know how hard you've worked for it, that first 'Chinese' or curry or the first pint after three months, when you've won and you're champion of the world, it's all worth it. To be honest if it wasn't worth it, you wouldn't do it would you?"

Ricky believes mental strength, in boxing or any other sport is as important as an athlete's physical attributes. So has he ever engaged the help of a psychologist or motivator? It seems to be en vogue for today's professional sportsmen and women.

His face couldn't look more disgusted if you accused him of being in love with Sir Alex Ferguson.

"If you have to be told to diet and train and go to bed early, you're not the champion or fighter you think you are. You shouldn't need people harpin' on at you."

He explains his own thought-processes when it comes to training.

"When I start training I focus on myself initially. As long as you've got the date, and you know you have to make the weight for that date, that's all you need to know. You don't even need to know who your opponent is.

"For the last six fights I've not struggled with my weight, but for this fight, moving up to welterweight I'm going to be jumping out of my skin.

"The minute the opponent's announced – that's when I start thinking about him. I won't watch tapes of Collazo for hours and hours but maybe for ten or 15 minutes a day.

"I put the tape in and see what he's good at and what I'm good at. He's a little fixation in my head.

"I don't want to think about him too much though – where yer head's battered. Just a bit, so it's always fresh in your memory what he does. You don't want to be watching the tapes all the time thinking – shit he is good, know what I mean?"

As Ricky laughs, his 'phone goes off. *Step On* by the Happy Mondays is his current ringtone.

If he beats Collazo in Boston, Ricky doesn't want to hang around. He wants a few more defining fights, then he can retire young, happy and rich.

The fight everyone wants to see is Hatton v Mayweather – a battle in which Ricky would start as underdog. That isn't a concern.

"Floyd Mayweather hasn't beat a Kostya Tszyu. Floyd Mayweather's won more titles at different weights, but he fought Corrales when he had boiled down to super-featherweight.

"He's fought people like Arturo Gatti and Manfredy who are easy to hit, DeMarcus Corley who's no great shakes, Sharmba Mitchell who's a bit washed up and Zab Judah who'd just lost to Boldimir.

"I'm not slagging him, he is what he is. He's won

titles at all the different weights and deserves to be number one pound-for-pound, but he hasn't beat Kostya Tszyu.

"I really believe that he's only number one pound-for-pound until he fights me. I really believe that.

"Floyd Mayweather's won world titles at super-feather, lightweight, light-welter and welter so he deserves to be number one. But only 'til he fights me.

"I believe that even more so after that fight against Judah. There's nothing to be scared about. It wasn't a bad performance, but it wasn't a great performance and it doesn't put the fear of God in me. But he is a class act."

Easter Sunday, 16 April......

No Easter eggs for Ricky.

Easter Monday, 17 April.........

1.50pm.....

The Phoenix Camp gym is busier than normal, not surprising as it's a Bank Holiday. There are about 20 people, mainly lads around 13 or 14 years old hanging around, wide-eyed as they watch Ricky in action.

At one point, Ricky has to dodge the bodies as he throws angry punches at one of the bags.

Despite this, he's still not tempted to close the doors of the gym, even occasionally.

"These are the people I like to have around me," he says as he takes a brief break. "This is the area I call home and no matter how many titles I win, I don't think I'll ever move out of the area.

"I don't have an entourage, hangers-on or patters-on-the-back and that. I'm very close to my family, I have a very tight-knit group of mates and if boxing finished tomorrow, the lads in the gym and Billy and Kerry would still be mates. That's the way I like it.

"None of my friends or family treat me as Ricky the world champion, or superstar, they treat me as

just Ricky. That's the way I like it and that's the way I am.

"I've always been a firm believer that if you're the best fighter in the world and everyone thinks you're an arrogant arsehole, I'd rather not be a champion."

Tuesday, 18 April......

It's Ricky's final day of training before sparring begins. One of Luis Collazo's former sparring partners is flying in from New York to help him prepare. Ricky will also be sparring with a Sheffield-based fighter next week.

When sparring starts it marks a step-up in training intensity. Ricky enjoys it although there are always risks involved.

"You generally don't get cut in sparring," he says. "It can happen, but you've got your big headguard, you get your Vaseline on and you're wearing the bigger gloves."

Ricky suffered with cuts above his left eye in the early part of his professional career. It was a real worry for Team Hatton until a visit to a Harley Street plastic surgeon uncovered a problem. An old wound had been stitched up with a ball of Vaseline still embedded inside. The eye was cleaned and 22 stiches inserted. The wound hasn't reopened since.

Injuries don't play on Ricky's mind. He enjoys sparring – no holds barred.

"It'll be sharp stuff, but we won't be taking liberties trying to knock each other out.

"I don't like doing rounds and rounds of sparring. A lot people go in for this touch-sparring, but no one's gonna just touch you when you get in the ring for the fight. You want it as realistic to the fight as possible, but without taking each other's head off. You don't wanna be in a fight before the fight.

"It has got out of hand a few times but generally I'm not a liberty taker. A couple of times it has happened though. Someone came down once and got a little bit flash, started to hold and spoil me a little bit, but generally it's alright.

"If someone like Junior Witter wants to come down to spar then there'd be a bit of needle there obviously. He can come down and spar as many times as he wants. Then he wouldn't want to fight me!"

Wednesday, 19 April......

City of Manchester Stadium......

11am......

Ricky's been invited to the City of Manchester Stadium to have his picture taken with the Barclays Premiership trophy which is on a tour of football grounds throughout the country. It seems his ties to City are nearly as strong as his association with boxing.

Chelsea are within touching distance of claiming the title ahead of their nearest rivals Manchester United. An unashamed 'bitter' Blue, Ricky holds up the trophy and poses for photos saying - "I'm glad I'm the only person in Manchester who'll be getting their hands on this!"

"I'm glad I'm the only person in Manchester who'll be getting their hands on this!"

(Pic. Paul Speak)

El Gato

The gym is especially busy. Word has spread about sparring and the new boy in town.

Frankie 'El Gato' Figueroa is working up a sweat dancing around one of the bags. The 27-year old Puerto Rican from the Bronx is dressed in a black 'Gleason's Gym' t-shirt, black tracksuit bottoms and a plugged in i-pod that's blocking out the chatter of the gym. He's in a world of his own.

He's short, about 5' 6 – an inch shorter than Ricky – and has a similar stocky frame. With a reputation for being a fast and tricky southpaw who's sparred with Collazo, Frankie is an obvious choice.

"I got the call last Thursday asking me if I wanted to come to England to spar with Ricky Hatton," he says in a rapid-fire 'New Yorican' accent. "I said, 'I'm on the plane already'. I'm honoured they selected me out of the whole nation.

"I'm here because I know I'm more slippery than Luis Collazo. I have quick hands and I want to prove to Hatton that if he can stop me then he can stop anybody."

He's keen and certainly isn't shy. Apparently his 'El Gato' (the cat) nickname comes from his ability to catch the cat which used to live at his old gym.

Kerry Kayes helps El Gato on with his protector, laces up his sparring gloves and manoeuvres his headguard into a comfortable position after taking off the i-pod.

At the far end of the room, Billy's getting Ricky – in shorts, no top - ready for action.

The pair get into the ring, touch gloves and start moving around each other. The only sound that can be heard is the background noise of Matthew Hatton grunting each time he makes contact with a bag. The sparring isn't going to get in the way of him finishing his own session.

Round one: Frankie's on the back-foot, moving around the ring in a low stance. He's awkward and slippy, but Ricky catches him a couple of times.

Round two: Frankie actually moves like a cat. He's always spinning around and hopping about. He manages to avoid most of Ricky's heavier blows, and catches Ricky with a good left on the nose – 'shot' Ricky shouts.

Round three: Billy Graham's calling Ricky's shots whilst leaning against the ropes. Ricky's finding his rhythm now and lands a couple of good left hooks to the body. Frankie has trouble with his headguard and heads to the corner where Paul Speak sorts him out.

Round four: Frankie's vocal now – 'this is what he'll do Hatton' – as he throws a left jab. Ricky finishes strongly to give Frankie a little taste of his power.

The buzzer sounds, the fighters embrace and pat each other on the head. The spectators applaud.

After a cool down, Frankie heads for the dressing room and starts to unlace his boots.

"Right now I'm 13-2 with ten knockouts. I'm very underrated and I'm here to prove a point to Ricky Hatton that I'm coming up.

"I want to showcase what you might not have here in Europe. Fast, slick fighters. I'm here to help Hatton take Collazo's title."

Frankie says he's had a rough career so far. His manager had no money so he's been forced to move around looking for fights in 'other guys' hometowns'.

"But I know what it takes to be a world champion," he insists.

"I have to be more of a boxer, I've learned that. But I only have short arms so it's kinda tough; y'understand what I'm sayin'? I'm the smallest in my division.

"But it's not about me; it's about Ricky Hatton. They've flown me out for some great sparring.

"I want to showcase what you might not have in Europe. Fast, slick fighters. I'm here to help Hatton take Collazo's title."

Frankie Figueroa

"Collazo will throw more jabs out, but the difference between me and Collazo is that I move more. By me moving it makes Hatton slip and weave and cut the ring off. It's almost identical to throwing a jab. You gotta slip and weave and cut the ring off.

"If Hatton knows how to slip and weave and avoid my punches, he's definitely gonna know how to avoid Collazo's jab.

"Ricky caught me with some good body shots, but I've got about an 80 percent defence. If you can block that many shots you're looking good in the game. If you block 90 percent like Winky Wright, you're great in the game.

"Hatton knows I'm no sucker. I'm gonna get caught, but I'm gonna give some back.

"I sparred with Arturo Gatti. We had a tremendous sparring session. I got Gatti thinking about boxers who can slip and weave."

Frankie likes to talk.

"So I'm sayin' to him in the ring – 'boom, boom, boom! That's what he does Hatton. That's what he does with those counter-shots'.

"I'm letting him know to get ready for that 'cos Collazo does that. He's pretty quick.

"It's about teamwork. Yes, I'm here to build Hatton's confidence up, that's what sparring partners do. But it's no good getting a sparring partner who'll beat you up. It makes no sense.

"If I catch Hatton, he'll sharpen up, and if he catches me, I'll sharpen up. That's called teamwork.

"I'm here to learn, you better believe it! I'm here to learn about Ricky Hatton's style. How does he throw a body hook and an uppercut? How does he jab? If a guy catches you with a shot, you gotta do it back."

What about his own fighting future?

"Even the greats like Frazier were sparring partners," he says as he flashes a big smile. "I'm here for the money, but by the same token there's fame I gotta get. I gotta get outta the hood, the Bronx.

"I got things I gotta do. So I honour Hatton for bringing me out here and showing me what a 40-0, 34-knockout dude can do!

"People say – 'why you wanna go over there? Why you wanna be a sparring partner?' Those people are wrong. If you close your mind as a boxer, you close your mind to your career.

"You gotta keep an open mind in every single thing you do. You have to take advice and play with it.

"After I finish here I'm gonna spar with Vivian Harris – ranked number seven in the world. I'm going there 'cos, one, I've no full-time job, and two, I'm learning. So then when I fight, I'm in tip-top shape."

Frankie's been put up in a hotel close to the gym. He's been in Manchester a day, and is enjoying the experience.

"In America people say the Europeans are very friendly. Man, they weren't lying! I'm a social person; I'll talk to anybody!" Thanks very much.

"Hatton is very down to earth. He's a friendly dude. I got off the plane and I got gifts of shirts and hats.

"I know he's a millionaire, but guys that have normally made money and are world champions, they don't do that. That's why I talk to people, 'cos people like Hatton, Floyd Mayweather and Arturo Gatti, they talk and it's real conversation.

"So it's definitely an honour to even get punched by Hatton, and throw a punch at Hatton."

2pm……

Ted Peate's in the gym again. He watched the sparring and is now busy drumming up support for an amateur boxing show he's organised for tomorrow night at Hyde Town Hall.

When his old mentor has gone, Ricky says, "I started boxing with Ted when I was 10 years of age, I'm 27 now so 17 years down the line and my old amateur coach still comes down here to see me and it's nice.

"The people you have around you in the early days set the basics in motion. There are a lot of people that helped me in those days.

"Obviously Ted was my first amateur coach, then after a couple of years I moved to the Sale West boxing club in Manchester under Paul Dunne.

"These are people you don't read about in the papers or watch on television; people that nobody hears of but they're just as important as those that are working with me today.

"They've all played their very important part. I still see them from time to time, they still come in the gym and they're never forgotten.

"I try my best to get up and see the kids at the amateur boxing clubs and speak to the coaches when I can. Sometimes months can go by where I don't speak to them which is unfortunate but I'm sure they appreciate how busy I am."

Tameside Lad

Thursday, 20 April......

Hyde Town Hall......

7.00pm......

A small queue has formed as friends and family of the young fighters wait to get in. Ted's on the door, resplendent in suit and tie, making sure the money's coming in.

A boxing ring's been put up in the middle of the big, recently refurbished hall. Seats have been set in rows of five or so around the ring, with plenty more room in the two long balconies running lengthways above. The bar in the room at the back is doing a brisk trade before the bouts begin.

Tonight's fighters range in age from 11 to 18. They're mainly from local clubs in Ashton-under-Lyne, Stockport, Hyde (Ted's Nichols Police Club) and a team have travelled from Kirkby on Merseyside.

Ricky's two oldest boxing friends, Tony Feno and Steve Bell are here.

"Me and Ricky first met when he was ten and I was 13. He was only a little tiny kid," says Steve.

"I remember the first day he came in the gym. I used to take the kids 'cos I could handle myself and I wouldn't take liberties with the young kids.

Ted Peate does his bit in the ring.

"I remember to this day, Ted said to me, 'take this young kid in the ring and see what he's like'. I was a lot bigger than Rick at the time and he came flying out, no fear, and started battering hell out of me. Straight away I thought, 'where has this kid come from?'

"Then he came to school and we kind of grew up together. Me, Rick and Feno was always together. We had a great laugh. We used to rip hell out of each other. We called ourselves the three amigos – Rick-os, Bell-os and Fe-nos."

Tony's now a fireman, while Steve is making a name for himself as a professional super-featherweight after a long, successful amateur career.

"Me and Ricky went to the ABAs in the same year which was good for us. Ricky turned pro the same year – '97. I sort of wanted to carry on and travel the world and do what I wanted to do as an amateur. I became England captain and all that.

"When I was a young kid I always said I wanted to win the ABAs and I won it twice. I wanted to box for England and I did 30 odd times and was captain of my country. So I've always achieved what I set out to do.

"I know for a fact, the one thing I want is a Lonsdale belt. I'd love a Lonsdale belt and I know I can win that. That's my goal for now and as soon as I get that then I'll see where I can go then."

If not the MGM in Las Vegas, then Hollywood will do. When not training, Steve has busied himself with a few small acting roles.

"I'll give myself another three years then hopefully get into acting and become a big film star!

"Since I turned pro I've had a lot more time. I had a part in Shameless. I played Donny McGuire. I head-butted a bloke. I've also got a part in Hollyoaks. I've been quite lucky when I've been out of training it's worked quite well for me."

Ricky once appeared in Coronation Street as an extra. He was playing type, having a pint in the rovers. It doesn't cut any ice with Belly.

"Yeah, he's done a bit in Corrie. He's shit though!"

8pm......

A couple of fights in, Ricky shows up. He's a bit late because of his obligatory evening run. His new mate Frankie is with him and the pair make their way to the stage overlooking the ring. A table has been set up. It's covered in medals and trophies which Ricky will present to the fighters over the course of the evening.

Ted's in the ring between each contest, announcing the result of the previous fight and calling up the next two fighters. He's struggling with the word 'unanimous.' After all these years, it's still either 'umanimous' or 'unaninous'.

Next up is a bout between one of his boxers and a kid from the Kirkby club. Ted can't resist making a crack about scousers and car tyres going missing.

One of the referees for the night is Georgio Brugnoli. The last time he officiated at a bout was at the Commonwealth Games in Melbourne last month, but, like most amateur boxing people, he

still turns up for these kind of shows wherever he's needed.

During the interval, Ricky heads for a quiet room at the back of the hall to grab a coffee. He spots a plate of sandwiches and wolfs down a beef salad. This isn't on Kerry's list, but Ricky explains he's dashed here straight from his run and hasn't had time to eat.

He still gets a buzz from the amateur nights.

"It's seeing the kids come up to you with smiles on their faces," he says after finishing the sandwich. "I remember how I was at their age.

"People like Carl Thompson, Chris Eubank and Barry McGuigan used to come to shows like this. It used to make your week. I'd like to think that's what they're thinking of me.

"When you're around eleven years of age, it's your world. I remember I lost my fifth fight and I wouldn't go out of the house for a week. I cried and cried and cried.

"You can tell how much the kids put in to it and it's brilliant really. A high percentage of these kids, if

Monday, 24 April......

Preparations are now cranked up a notch. Today marks the start of two hard weeks' training before Ricky leaves for Boston.

12.40pm......

After a good warm-up, the day begins with six, three-minute rounds on the heavy bag followed by six rounds of jumping the bar. Next up – six rounds of sparring with Frankie, six rounds on the belt with Billy and twenty minutes lifting heavy weights with Kerry (quadriceps).

3.10pm......

Ricky feels good. He's handled the step up in training intensity with no problems. He's now sitting in the canteen having a brew with Kerry and Frankie.

The Phoenix Camp Gym has proved to be a real eye-opener for Frankie. He's enjoying working with everyone and will head home with some new ideas.

"I got so much trust in Kerry," he says while hungrily eyeing a plate of battered fish being devoured by a bodybuilder on the table next to him.

"He's been instructing me in nutrition and I've got so much belief in what he says, so like Ricky, I've been taking the multi-vitamins and having the recovery shakes. I never used to use all this, but I will now."

A high-school wrestler before he got into boxing, Frankie still can't get his head around some other Manchester methods. Weightlifting is still a mystery to him, "I only look at 'em. I come from that background."

But he's learned more than he'd bargained for in his short time in England.

"When I go back home I wanna get a fitness coach, and use Kerry's supplements. When I next fight somebody, I wanna be over-matched. I wanna make money easy – I don't wanna get hit.

"I'm lovin' it here. I love this place, it's amazing."

Ricky has his head in the paper. There's obviously an interesting article on page three as he's in a world of his own. After a short while he tunes into the conversation and picks up on Frankie's thoughts about diet and supplements.

"Nutrition was my Achilles heel," he says with a nod. "Sometimes out of the gym I let myself go a little too much.

"I was doing okay before I hooked up with Kerry, I was unbeaten and doing alright, but sometimes at the very top level it can be the little things that make a difference. A little bit of improved nutrition, a bit of extra weight training. Sometimes you're so well matched with your opponent that these little things can be the difference between winning and losing.

"That was the difference with Kostya Tszyu. I was that little bit fitter, a bit stronger and maybe I'd had a bit better nutrition. In a fight that's so nip and tuck, that made the difference in the end.

"There's a fine line between winning and losing at the very top level."

Kerry's been quiet so far, scribbling on a piece of paper. He's worked it out now: "He [Ricky] has just lifted, on that last leg workout, twenty eight and a half tonne!" He proclaims, proud of his charge.

"I thought my balls were gonna pop outta my ears!" says the star pupil.

Kerry continues: "I was the British Champion [bodybuilder] and there was a bit more involved for me. We have to remember that Ricky's training for boxing so we have to condense it. But as British Champion I never did that!"

"It's like lifting those tits!" Ricky laughs as he points to a buxom young lady in *The Sun*.

Kerry keeps his train of thought: "His last set of ten reps was more than two Rolls Royces!"

As Kerry continues with his calculations, Ricky tells Frankie all about their weights routine, how he focuses on a couple of body parts each day and how he feels so much faster in the ring now as a result. Frankie looks surprised.

"Boxing's a sport, but there are still so many people doing it old school," Ricky argues. "A lot of boxers are still chasing chickens and eating raw eggs in the morning!"

"Raw eggs are the worst thing you can eat!" Kerry adds seriously.

The chat continues. Ricky says it's been good having Frankie around.

"He came very highly recommended and

everything we were told has turned out true. He has every chance of making it in the division himself. Even though he's over here as a sparring partner, he shouldn't be labelled as just a sparring partner, he's a contender in his own right, know what I mean?

"In my career I've had 40 fights and I think I've boxed about four southpaws. The last time I fought a southpaw was two years ago so coming in and sparring with southpaws was something new to me.

"The first session with Frankie was a bit of a struggle. I felt a little bit uncomfortable but I'm quite happy with how well I've got used to him. I usually work out an opponent pretty quick. I think that's one of my qualities.

"I'm known as a 100-mile-an-hour fighter and body-puncher but I'm a little bit cleverer than that. So I've adjusted to the sparring quite well considering I haven't fought a southpaw for so long.

"Frankie's caused me plenty of problems. So many times I've had sparring partners who haven't caused me any problems and there's no point in having it all your own way."

The subject of Frankie's nickname arises. He shows everyone around the table the tattoo of a vicious looking cat on his left arm.

Ricky admits he's terrified of cats.

"Kerry bought me a stuffed cat to put on my fireplace."

"I didn't know did I?" Kerry pleads.

After flashing Kerry an evil look, Ricky picks up again: "I'm not allergic, I'm just scared of 'em. I got scratched by one right down the face when I was about one year old. Now when I see 'em, I'm proper scared.

"But anyway, Kerry bought me this stuffed cat and I thought, there's no way I'm having that in my house. Then Campbell walked in and said – 'Oh is that for me dad?' So I've got to keep it in the house."

Back to his paper as everyone else continues sipping warm tea or coffee while commenting on the weather. It's been raining would you believe.

All of a sudden Ricky pipes up again, "I was reading a few weeks back about that Gavin Henson, you know who goes out with Charlotte Church. He has to put his false tan on before he plays! I've never heard so much shit!

"I'd never ever do that. I wanna be known as the great white hope!"

" I'm not allergic to cats, I'm just scared of 'em!

I got scratched by one right down the face when I was about one year old. Now when I see 'em, I'm proper scared."

Gee Cross, Hyde......

8pm......

The door to Ricky's house is opened by Jennifer, his friendly, pretty, brunette girlfriend.

Ricky is stood in the middle of his living/games room piling on layers of clothes in preparation for his nightly run. He's wearing trainers, sweatsuit bottoms, a t-shirt, three sweatshirts and a rain jacket.

"I like to wear a lot of clothes to weigh me down a bit and make it harder," he explains.

Before he leaves the house, he points out some of his favourite memorabilia on the wall. Jennifer is trying to watch Eastenders.

Pride of place is a First Division winners medal which was given to him by the then Manchester City boss Kevin Keegan.

"He actually gave me his own medal!" Ricky says, still sounding surprised.

There are signed pictures of movie stars and his sporting heroes – there's even an original poster signed by Elvis from his film *Girls, Girls, Girls*.

He's nearly ready to run – just the i-pod to sort out first. He's getting the right tunes lined up.

"I like a bit of Stone Roses, Oasis or the Chillies when I'm running."

Then, with woolly hat pulled over the ears, he's off on his lonely run. He leaves his house in Gee Cross, turns right at the bottom of his street and heads down the winding main road towards the Hattersley estate.

Only fields, and about two miles, separate Gee Cross and Hattersley. It's easy to see how he was so spooked when he was running in the middle of the night whilst training for the Kostya Tszyu fight.

The Celebrity

Tuesday, 25 April......

1.30pm......

Frankie's in the gym but he's not training. He wasn't due to spar today, but he's out of action in any case as he says he injured his left shoulder in a fall in the ring yesterday.

Ricky's on the belt with Billy who's telling him to move from an orthodox stance to southpaw and back again. El Gato's perched on a window-sill taking it all in.

2.20pm......

After Kerry puts Ricky through the usual 20 minutes of weightlifting (Tuesday = chest and biceps), he makes his way to his favourite step machine. It's the one nearest the canteen counter and the exit - probably Ricky's two favourite features of the gym.

Ricky's doing his usual, pumping his legs while singing along to whatever tune's being played. He stops singing for a second. One of the muscle-bound creatures is attempting to lift a bar with what looks like a small mountain balanced on either end. Ricky shouts his encouragement - or piss-take as it's otherwise known.

2.25pm......

There are five lads, about 15 years old, who've been hanging around watching training for the last couple of hours. They're not just here to see Ricky. They've heard cricket hero Andrew 'Freddie' Flintoff will be in the gym today.

The current England captain is due to film an item called 'Ready, Steady, Freddie' for Sky's *Cricket AM* programme.
It involves the big man meeting other athletes, having a laugh and picking up tips on how to make it in their respective sports.

As he pounds away on the step machine, Ricky says he's looking forward to seeing Freddie again, someone he's met socially on a couple of occasions.

"I'm gonna show him some moves," he says. "He's sound, dead down to earth. A crackin' fella. He's a big f****r though. If he hits me............."

The big f****r walks through the door of Betta Bodies with a camera crew while Ricky's still on the stepper. They pair quickly shake hands and share a joke before Freddie heads off to get changed.

Freddie walks out of the changing rooms wearing a navy Lonsdale 'Hitman' t-shirt and a huge pair of boxing shorts sporting a St George Cross.

Speaky hands Ricky a new pair of his specially made spangly, fight-night shorts to put on for the cameras. He's not happy with the colour – reckons there's too much red in them.

Both sportsmen then sit on the ring apron while Ricky shows Freddie how to bandage his hands. Gloves on, then it's into the ring for a bit of touching around with Ricky on the pads.

At 6'5" Flintoff is indeed big and he looks in great shape. Ricky's shouting at him, 'left jab, and again, right cross'. Freddie holds himself well and looks like he could have been a half-decent heavyweight. He's seen the inside of a boxing gym before.

Ricky's been in this situation before. Other well known boxing fans have climbed through the ropes at the Phoenix Camp.

City boss Stuart Pearce is one of them. Looking back at the experience, he said, "I went to watch Ricky train at the gym and I got in the ring with him.

"I tell you what: it's a bloody lonely place in the ring. I shit myself in there. You're facing a boxer with a set of gloves and you think, 'there's nowhere to hide in this ring'.

"I knew he weren't gonna hit me, he may give me a tap on the chin, but he weren't gonna clock me. But I tell you what, one or two people from various walks of life or professions should get in there.

"It makes you realise you're very privileged to be a footballer because look at the alternatives you might have in other sports – get in a ring and see how daunting it is!"

Freddie seems to be enjoying himself though. Next up is the body-belt with the big cricketer playing Billy. The buzzer on the wall sounds and Ricky tears into him, forcing Freddie onto the ropes

(Pic. Paul Speak)

in a controlled frenzy. The Sky director's face is a picture. One false move and the great Ashes hero could be hospitalised – and it would be all his fault!

No harm done. Freddie clambers through the ropes for a session of jumping the bar before finishing off on the bags.

Session over, Ricky and Freddie catch their breath on the ring apron and chat about how the last time they'd met it was in Manchester's legendary, open-all-hours, Press Club. They'd had a few.

Like Ricky, Freddie has had weight issues throughout his career, but says he's benefited from boxing training.

"I trained in Salford for a while in Oliver's gym with Jamie Moore and Anthony Farnell," he says now breathing normally. "But it's great coming here 'cos I'm a fan of Ricky. I watch his fights.

"It was great getting that big belt on and he's in front of you whacking away so hard! It didn't hurt but you can feel it. You're certainly aware there's something hitting you! It's the speed, and he's all over you. If I didn't have that belt on I'd have been on my back!

"At Oliver's I was doing a bit on the bag and the bar work. A lot of it was stamina and I did a little bit in the ring as well.

"It was good because with cricket and boxing, although they're two different sports, there are a couple of parallels. There's the hand-eye co-ordination and a side-on view.

"I've found I'm now a lot lighter on my feet and a lot stronger and I've been doing the skipping just to stay light."

"The discipline these boxing lads have is amazing. All the training and how fit they are. You have a go at jumping the bar, then a minute in the ring, then hitting some pads, it's tough work!

tries a flashy little spin to avoid a Hatton hook. Ricky the Showman can't resist taking the piss and does the same, slapping Frankie with the back of his glove in the process. The punters love it, Frankie smiles and Billy shouts, "That's how we do it in Manchester!"

2.50pm......

Billy appears to be in a good mood. He's now finished with all three fighters for the day. His office is filled with smoke – Liston's a five-a-day iguana – and there are a couple of Billy's mates sitting on the sofa.

He likes what he's seen today. Ricky's settled into his sparring.

"Frankie's very fast and shifty and I think he fancies his chances against the top light-welterweights," Billy says. "He did fancy his chances against Ricky but I think he's changed his mind after a few days. That generally tends to

happen when anybody comes over here to spar.

"But Frankie is fast and clever, he's sparred with all the top people in the world and that's why we got him in. But he's getting a little bit tired now, he's got niggles and that. I don't know how bad they are like, but I don't think Ricky's gonna get much more out of Frankie. He has served a purpose though.

"The other kid [Manoo] - I need him big for next week. He's quite a lot like Collazo. He can hit as well. That makes Ricky more aware and makes him perform better. He needs a bit of danger. He can get a little bit lackadaisical at times like he did last week when he first started sparring.

"Frankie hasn't got the firepower to really hurt Ricky, so what happens with him, as with a lot of fighters, they don't use as much effort, you know what I mean? If it's not dangerous you can get a little bit loose and the anticipation isn't quite as good 'cos the nerves aren't there.

"The only people you can get to spar with Ricky, around his weight, are the best men in the world and obviously you're not gonna get them. The only time they want to share a ring with Ricky Hatton is when they're gettin' paid loadsa money to fight for a title. But they're the only people who can be really competitive with Ricky Hatton over a few rounds, so we have to get bigger kids in.

"The second kid [Manoo] is the same height [as Collazo] only he's bigger and heavy-handed. He's very clever and he's had loads and loads of amateur fights. He knows his way around and we're gonna need him.

"He's a vastly experienced amateur, now he's turned pro. He's in his thirties and is really seasoned. He holds himself quite a lot like Collazo so he's bang on.

"I've seen what I wanted to see today and I'll go home really happy. It's always the same: when Ricky first starts sparring I watch and see what's gone a little bit out of synch, what's wrong, and then start to put it right. But we've been together now for an awful long time and prepared for title fights – it seems for ever – so we know the score, know what I mean? Today it's all come alive and we're really gonna get somewhere next week."

It's fast and furious stuff. Billy finally draws breath with the aid of a Benson & Hedges

"Ricky's bang on time. Your moods keep changing when you're preparing for a fight. You might put on a tape and it'll make you feel really good. Other days you'll look at the tape and think it's going to be a bit tricky. Sometimes you go home and think 'there's gonna be problems this time', you know what I mean?

"I've always been certain Ricky can beat him [Collazo], he can beat anyone around his weight in the world, but I'd have to be stupid to go looking for a southpaw. He's a welterweight and a southpaw so he's gonna cause problems for the first few rounds. But I've never doubted Ricky Hatton will win the fight.

"I never count my chickens. I always look at the worst case scenario because anything else is then a bonus. You've got to keep yer head right. You can't get complacent. I prepare for the worst thing to happen."

Talk switches to Boston. Team Hatton is due to arrive in the US just a week before the fight as Ricky doesn't like being away from home for too long. That's fine with Billy.

"Ricky's a Manchester kid; he likes to train in this area. Me, personally, I don't care where I am.

"All the work will be done, so the last week we'll spend just looking at tactics and that, and making the weight.

"Ricky's an entertainer, and I'm a bit like that meself. I'm looking forward to going over there and showing the American public and the people of Boston how good my kid is. You know what I mean? It's kinda excitin'.

"It won't make any difference being over there. A ring's a ring and Ricky thrives under pressure to be honest with ya. I think I must do meself."

What of the other two fighters in the gym? Matthew Macklin returned to the gym this week after spending time at home in Birmingham following the postponement of his fight with Jamie Moore. He's now pencilled in for another fight on 1 June in his hometown.

Even though he's not fighting in the States, Macklin will be there as part of Team Hatton.

"I'm really excited about his career," Billy says. "I think it's gonna be a great ride with Matthew Macklin. I see something a little bit special and he fights with loads of passion. The same as Ricky Hatton does. That's what makes them stand out."

Matthew Hatton is fighting in Boston, on Ricky's undercard. What does Billy know about his opponent.

"Well, we know his record and stuff like that," he says as he perches himself on the edge of the office table. "You're never gonna find out much, you try and find out as much as you can, but you're not gonna find out too much."

Billy knows Matthew's opponent's record and has been trying to find out as much as possible. So what's the opponent's name?

"I don't know his f***** name!" Billy snaps, eyes bulging. "How would I know his f***** name? I don't know his f***** name!

"I've been told his f***** name but I've forgotten his f***** name! I know his record and that's more important to me!"

Silly f***** question obviously.

Billy switches instantly back to happy mode when the chat moves on to how Matthew's career is going.

"He's performing better in the gym," he says with a nod of his shaven head, "he's sharper, he's coming on nicely. People put too much pressure on Matthew Hatton. He was an 18 year old novice when he come to me and he's really applied himself.

"Some people got a little bit frustrated with him at times, but I never did 'cos I knew from the off it'd take time. It's all come together for him now and he's really improved.

"But you know, everyone knows Ricky's the man. It's his time. It's the most important time of his career so he obviously takes priority.

"I've only got a few fighters now and it's how I like it. I'm really enjoying meself now. I've got a load of enthusiasm and I feel brand new to be honest with ya. I'm excited by everything what's goin' on now.

"It's gonna be the hardest times with me and Ricky Hatton, but the best times. It's the most glory, the most money, so these are the most important times."

Thursday, 27 April......

Freddie Flintoff's visit to the gym with a film crew two days ago highlights the fact that Ricky, for all his boy next door earthiness, is an elite sporting 'celebrity'.

He's been asked to appear on reality TV shows but has so far declined, unlike his old nemesis Kostya Tszyu who's been wooing Australia with his fancy footwork on *Dancing with the Stars*.

Ricky ponders for a few seconds, and says: "Well, Kostya Tszyu is a star down there. Without meaning to sound disrespectful, they've only really got a few.

"You've got Kostya Tszyu and the tennis star Leyton Hewitt. Kostya's doing 'come dancing' or whatever, well why not? He is a superstar, one of the best light-welterweights of all time."

So far, Ricky's limited his TV appearances to

sporting quiz shows, an appearance on the BBC's *Superstars*, and a walk-on part in *Coronation Street*.

"There's *An Audience with Coronation Street* coming up," he says. "I've been invited to that but I can't go with the fight coming up.

"Everyone that I've met from Corrie – Andy Whymet, Stevie Arnold, Martin Platt, Tyrone – there's not one that I've thought, 'he's an arsehole or whatever'. They're all nice genuine people.

"You always expect high-profile people from TV to be a bit big-time or whatever, but the ones I know aren't like that.

"I'm not really a VIP merchant though. Some people would jump at the chance of going down the red carpet, but I'd be a bit embarrassed.

"Sometimes I do go into Manchester – but not the places to go to if you know what I mean. I'm certainly not one of the faces. I'm happier having a pint in one of the Wetherspoons.

"I do get quite a bit of attention, but it doesn't bother me. People come up and say, 'hi Rick, can we have a picture?' I say, 'yeah, no problem'.

"It's only been on a few occasions I've thought, 'this is a bit much.'

"I was in Marbella after the Kostya Tszyu fight. I walked into Lineker's bar and they were all over me. Someone pulled me gold chain off! I thought, 'whoa, Jesus, this is bit much!'

"But generally it's not like that because I am pretty approachable. No one gets smart."

Friday, 28 April......

1.05pm......

The gym's busy again with onlookers standing all around the ring. Matthew Macklin and Matthew Hatton provide the warm-up spar as ex-Manchester City and Sunderland winger Nicky Summerbee looks on with his little boy. Salford's Steve 'the Viking' Foster – a former world middleweight contender – is also here.

The two Matthews finish their four rounds and Ricky and Manoo take over. Again, it's captivating with Manoo trying to land big shots, Ricky moving well and catching the Iranian with a couple of rib ticklers.

After six rounds, Frankie replaces Manoo, but Ricky grimaces as he misses with a right uppercut. At the end of round one, he's still in pain. Billy and Kerry have a look at his elbow, and decide to cut sparring short.

Ricky's tweaked an old injury but it isn't serious enough for him to miss out on a few rounds with Billy on the pads.

During a break, he spots one of his major sponsors, Ged Mason of Morson. He takes a big slug of water and wanders to the ropes near where Ged is standing. As Ged looks up to say hello, Ricky uneashes his mouthful. He can fit a lot of water in that mouth of his.

A soaked Ged Mason   (Pic James McGoff)

Blue Heaven (or Hell)

Saturday, 29 April......

Two weeks to fight-night......

City of Manchester Stadium

2.40pm......

Manchester City v Fulham. Ricky has Campbell on his shoulders and his dad Ray alongside him as he makes his way towards the executive entrance of the stadium.

Before he can make it through the doors, Ricky's been spotted and a group of lads want autographs. He happily obliges and poses for a few mobile phone pictures before heading into the ground.

In the lift on the way up to his box, the talk is about Manchester United and Wayne Rooney. United have lost 3-0 away at Chelsea in the lunchtime kick-off – a defeat which confirms the Londoners as Premiership Champions and makes Ricky very happy.

But his glee is tempered by news of a bad injury to Rooney. Hated of course when wearing the red of United, but he's England's great talisman and the World Cup's just around the corner.

3.00pm......

Ricky and friends take to their seats outside. There's a real end of season, muted atmosphere about the place – neither side has anything to play for and the ground looks half-empty. But Ricky's just happy to get away from it all for the next couple of hours.

"We've not had a lot of home games lately," he says, "but the last few we have had I've missed them unfortunately. I've had an event on or something, so it's nice to come back and watch the lads again."

3.08pm......

He's out of his seat now as a long pass goes astray – "rubbish City.....rubbish!" He calmly sits back down again after venting his fury.

"Chelsea have won the league today which is good," he says, now back in a happy place. "If we're not gonna win nowt, you just don't want United to win anything.

"I'm a little bit disappointed about Rooney getting stretchered off. Even the most hardened of City fans will be worried about that with the World Cup coming up. I know I am, so hopefully he makes a good recovery."

Campbell, who's wearing a Man City coat, is more interested in playing with his dad and granddad than watching the Blues. He's climbing all over Ricky who's trying to multi-task.

"It's important that I bring him [Campbell]. You've got to set kids at a young age on the right road!" He laughs. "Being at City, there's no better education really. But he is a little bit brainwashed in a way. Brainwashed for the better."

City old-boy Mike Summerbee turns up for a chat while doing his rounds, saying hello to the supporters in the corporate boxes.

"We've become good friends with Mike over the years, and he remembers my dad from when he used to play football with him. Every game he calls in our box and has a few words. He's always in the gym as well. He's a good bloke.

"As you know, Nicky Summerbee comes down the gym as well. In fact that was the last good City team we had when Nicky was playing. We had Rosler and Walsh up front, Beagrie on the right wing, Summerbee on the left wing. I think that was the best team we've had in recent years really." The football's dull. Back to boxing. Is that elbow injury a problem?

"I've had trouble with my elbow the last couple of fights," Ricky explains, "but I've been a little bit

lazy. I should have gone to the physio but I've been able to just get through the training.

"The minute I had the slightest little twinge I should have nipped it in the bud straight away, but because I've been getting away with it, it hurt that little bit more than it has in previous training camps.

"I've been to the physio, and he's not worried about it. It's more of a precaution than anything. I'm not worried.

"To be honest, as far as injuries go in my career,

I've had knuckles and elbows and stuff like that, but I've been very, very fortunate. I can't complain at all.

"On the night I could probably fight through the pain barrier, but I must admit it was very painful yesterday. I've got another fortnight to have treatment on it so I'm not worried.

"Otherwise, training couldn't be going better. Sparring yesterday I felt fantastic. I felt really sharp and really on form.

"I hurt my arm, but after a few minutes I was on

Liston the lizard

'Mayday'

Monday, 1 May......

12.30pm......

A fatality at the Phoenix Camp Gym has been narrowly avoided. Billy opened up as normal after the weekend to find Liston the iguana distinctly unwell. The room was not of the required temperature to keep a reptile, native to Central or South America, healthy.

And it's all Ricky Hatton's fault – a man living up to his 'Hitman' monicker.

"Well I was getting weighed on Friday and there's a heater in the tank where the lizard is," Ricky says, sadly shaking his head with shame at the retelling of the sorry tale.

"Obviously I pulled out the plug for the radiator so I could put the electric scales on and I forgot to put the radiator back on!" At this, Ricky throws back his head and bursts out laughing. After a few seconds he continues.

"Billy come in today and the lizard was shivering to f***!"

He's properly giggling now. Eventually he gets a grip.

"Billy wasn't too happy. I could see he wasn't too happy! "I didn't realise it was the plug for the lizard's radiator. When I get weighed tomorrow I'll have to be careful. If anything happens to Billy's lizards or his frogs or snakes, the world comes to an end."

1.00pm......

It's Ricky's final sparring session. It's a Bank Holiday and the gym is packed. *The Importance of being Idle* by Oasis is blaring over the stereo and both Ricky and Manoo work away on the bags before colliding in the ring one last time.

Frankie's a spectator today, his job's now finished and he leaves for home in the morning.

"I've found this trip very phenomenal," he says. "It's been an honour and a pleasure. It's been a real worthwhile adventure coming to Manchester, England.

"When I think of training camps I think of isolation. I think of hotels and they'll call me when they're ready. Not visiting sights, not mingling with the locals, being taken to local boxing clubs and shown different things. I didn't think it'd be like that.

"My expectations of England have surpassed what I thought before I came here. I'm glad I came.

"The Hatton family, everybody, they all looked after me. I didn't have to pay for respect as you'd sometimes have to do in America. There was respect everywhere.

"I definitely plan to get to Boston and support Ricky in this case 'cos I did help him out. I was here in preparations for Hatton, but I'm still a friend of Callazo."

So who do you think...? Frankie sees the inevitable question coming and starts to answer before the sentence is complete.

"My prediction? I want both guys to win!

"I like styles. Styles make fights. Collazo has the kinda style that can beat an aggressive boxer, but an aggressive boxer will tire out a boxer if he's not in top condition for 12 rounds.

"You don't want to see two boxers, or two aggressors. This is boxer against aggressor and whoever has the better conditioning will win.

"I can't really say too much about Collazo – that was two years ago. He's a world champion now and his training won't be what it was two years ago. I know then, he was very much an aggressor. But when he had his first defence, he was a boxer.

"Ricky Hatton is an aggressor. Very much an aggressor."

But isn't Ricky a better boxer than people give him credit for?

"No. He's a majority of an aggressor. Boxers stay on the outside, Hatton doesn't really stay on the outside. If he is on the outside, it's so he can figure out how to get in.

"Boxers need to use the whole ring. Hatton doesn't use the whole ring. He'll stay on the inside and that's not boxing, it's called weaving and ducking. Hatton didn't box me."

El Gato is now looking forward to ten days at home before he flies out to help Vivian Harris train for his forthcoming fight with Mike Arnaoutis.

After that, Frankie says there'll be no more sparring for anybody, it'll be Frankie time.

This bubbly New Yorker's made new friends in England and he can't wait to tell the folks back home all about it.

"Sparring with Ricky Hatton was phenomenal, but getting respect over here when you guys didn't know too much about me, that's what I like the most."

1.30pm........

Men, women and children are hemmed in around the ring. Those at the back are craning their necks for a decent view as the two fighters trade blows. Ricky's giving that little bit more today – certainly no sign of a problem with that troublesome elbow. He's looking strong and lands a couple of sharp body shots – there's a sickening slap as he finds Manoo's ribs.

But Manoo's tough and he keeps coming back for more. The fighters are sweating nearly as much as the punters watching. The gym's always hot, but it's a glorious day outside and the sun's burning in through the windows, adding to the rising temperature from the extra bodies and the full-on radiators.

The sparring session ends with a flurry of punches from both fighters – Ricky's strength evident despite his physical disadvantage.

2.20pm........

Manoo's showered and changed. He's packing his kit-bag in the dressing room. Now 31, he's been in England for five years. He turned professional in November last year after a long amateur career. He says he had 150-200 fights, "something like that."

(Pic. courtesy of Dominic Ingle)

So far he's had five pro fights, won three, drawn two. He's not happy about the draws. His next fight – against Geard Ajetovic of Serbia – is on 13 May on the Clinton Woods undercard, in Sheffield.

"Everything is going well, especially now I have sparred with Ricky Hatton," Manoo says with a big smile. "It was big experience for me. I respect him and it was big opportunity for me to spar with somebody who is world champion and one of the best in the world.

"I was a fan of Ricky Hatton and now have fingers crossed for Ricky Hatton.

"To be honest, people say to me I'm a strong boxer. When I'm fighting I am strong, but I tell you, Ricky Hatton is really strong!

"I couldn't fight with him, you know? I had to box with him. At his size I am just surprised how a person can have so much power.

"I turned pro late. I had a couple of problems in my life but now those problems are over. Now I'm in good shape and I believe in myself.

"After sparring with Ricky Hatton I'm more confident and if everything goes right for me I think I can be a future world champion.

"If Ricky Hatton can't knock me out then nobody can. His punches are very strong but my body is very strong. I'm good at taking very heavy shots. Ricky Hatton put in some very good body shots but I was okay. He punches very strong and I could feel them. Yeah!"

Manoo cannot hide his delight at being knocked around a boxing ring by Ricky Hatton. Life hasn't been easy for him and he's been touched by the generosity shown to him by Team Hatton, and especially Ricky.

"He's very lovely guy. I said before he was good world champion and I'd love to meet him 'cos he's very nice person.

"I saw when he gave his belt to his father. It made me cry you know because I haven't seen my family for more than six years. I could feel how much Ricky Hatton loves his father.

"He is world champion, he is rich, he could say, 'I'm not bothered about anybody' but he present that belt to his father and said, 'my father is world champion'. I love his personality.

"I will see my family this summer definitely. They come over here. Now I'm married to British girl and have baby son so I have family here. I love England 'cos it gives me this opportunity to prove myself."

Tuesday, 2 May......

Midday......

A camera crew has arrived to conduct an interview for Canadian TV. Members of Her Majesty's press and an American journalist are also in town.

Whilst sitting on the ring apron, making notes, I sense someone moving rapidly towards me. I look up and a powerful jet of water hits me in the eyes. My hair and face are soaked as water trickles onto my shirt.

12.20pm......

Kevin Dupont from the Boston Globe has flown into Manchester this morning. He says his home city is looking forward to Ricky's 'American Invasion'.

"We haven't had a named fighter in Boston that people have been engaged in since Hagler," he says. "A lot has happened since then to the city and to Hagler.

"Where Marvin used to fight was the old Boston Garden which was steeped in history and went back to the 1920s. When the original arena was built it was built principally for boxing and for ice hockey.

"It was an arena of 14 thousand but it had great steep side angles so when you went to boxing or hockey, even if you had cheap seats, you were right over it. You had this intimate connection.

"The town has waited a good long time for memorable events to come into the place."

British fans heading over for the fight are, apparently, sure to enjoy the sights and sounds of the city.

"It's a great time of year to be in Boston. The city is blossoming 'cos of spring time. And it's always good for drinking. Maybe too good some times!"

But will American fight fans come out in force to watch the British Hitman?

Kevin's not so sure, "Ricky is huge here but I don't get the sense that he is at home. Boxing in America has been so riddled with scandals and constant bickering between rival factions, stories of boxers' earnings being run-off by the manager.

"Boxing now in America and to a greater extent in Boston, is not on the map because of its own image and because Vegas takes so many of the fights.

"My feeling has always been that if the fighter is exciting then people will get caught up in it. But I don't get the sense that Bostonians know him yet.

"The HBO thing helps, but I'll be curious to see if they sell it out. I've been reading that three to five thousand people will travel over, which I find astonishing."

12.50pm......

Ricky's on the second day of the second 'hard' week in the run up to the fight. No sparring or weightlifting now, just bags, bar, body-belt and running.

2.15pm......

An as-live interview with Canadian TV is underway. Ricky's sitting in front of a camera at the side of the ring as questions are fired at him from the anchorman in Toronto.

Q: Collazo's a southpaw – how will you fight him?

RH: I'll cut the ring down, move in quickly. He's a very good technical boxer so I don't want to just steam in. I believe I'm up to the job. I'm very versatile.

Q: What's the situation with you and Frank Warren?

RH: I don't want to talk too much about it. That's in the past and I want to look to the future, and that future is taking the belt off Luis Collazo.

Q: So the case is over right?

RH: Not particularly, no. There was a court date set for, funnily enough, the Monday after the fight. It was a bit of an inconvenience but I was still willing to go ahead with it even though it was just two days after my fight.

The sooner we get a date and get it sorted the better. I'd sooner people were writing about Ricky Hatton winning championships rather than reading about Ricky Hatton being in court.

Training and media commitments are now over for the day. Ricky's signing photographs and boxing gloves for Paul Speak, who's also showing off the new 'Team Hitman' kit for Boston he's just had delivered.

As Paul is holding up each t-shirt and sweatshirt - like a model from the Price is Right, but not so easy on the eye - his mobile phone goes off. The ring-tone is the instantly recognisable theme from the film *Rocky* (not *Eye of the Tiger*, the other one).

Ricky's not impressed. He's heard it too many times, "will you change that f****** tone! How corny is that?"

(Pic. courtesy of Dominic Ingle)

"When he gave his belt to his father it made me cry because I haven't seen my family for more than six years. I could feel how much Ricky Hatton loves his father."

Manoo Salari

Wednesday, 3 May......

City of Manchester Stadium......

Press Conference......

11am......

TV crews, radio journalists and the writers from the national press are all here in the Mancunian Suite awaiting the arrival of the top table guests.

From left to right they take their seats - Billy Graham, Ray Hatton, Robert Waterman, Ricky Hatton, Clinton Woods, Dennis Hobson, Richard Poxon (Woods trainer), Gareth Williams.

It's the press conference to publicise Fight Academy's double bill on May 13. The fun starts in Sheffield with the 'Meltdown' promotion and a headlining rematch between hometown boy and IBF light-heavyweight title holder, Clinton Woods, and Jason DeLisle of Australia.

The second part of the bill is the 'Hitman Invasion'.

Dennis Hobson introduces everyone and gets the formalities out of the way. Ricky and Clinton say their bit before the floor is opened for questions.

The press want to know if the WBA have sanctioned the fight yet in the wake of Souleymane M'baye's legal bid. Gareth Williams deals with this. The answer is 'not yet' but the solicitor and the promoters are confident all will be sorted in due course.

The upshot is, if the WBA fail to sanction the bout, it will still go ahead as a non-title contest.

This subject dominates the press conference.

Billy offers up a few gems including, "We all know about boxing politics. It's all bollocks! Politics bollocks!"

When the questions do get to the boxing, Ray Hatton chips in saying, "Ricky's waited a long time to make his debut as a recognised champion in America and we've had a lot of problems outside the ring and it's all behind us now.

"He wants to go over there, do himself proud and do the people of Manchester and Great Britain proud."

Ricky's asked about Collazo's greater reach, "It's not about how many inches you've got," he says with a 'Carry On' grin.

Maybe Ricky remembers the pretty young woman who walked into a pub and asked for a 'double entendre'.......so the barman gave her one!

After the formal press conference, Ricky breaks away to give interviews to the various TV crews, radio and written press.

Midday......

Ricky moves out of the suite and into the foyer where he poses for photos in front of a Union Flag, pot of tea in hand. He's heading to Boston after all.

12.30pm......

Team Hatton leaves the stadium and heads east down Hyde Road for the 15 minute drive to Denton.

1.30pm......

As Ricky gets his mind back on training after his morning media commitments, Kerry Kayes makes his entrance. His strength work with Ricky is now finished but he still has plenty to do.

"The way I see it I've got three jobs," he says. "The first job is to get his body down to a weight that him and Billy are happy with after the two weeks of hard training. I believe I've done that job.

"In bringing him down we had to lose the same amount of body fat but give him extra muscle on his physique. Now that the body fat is down, you can noticeably see the extra muscle. With the extra muscle you can see all the explosive power he's got in the ring.

"The second job is to get him back on the scales at ten-seven at the weigh-in, and the third job is to get him in the ring at a heavier weight – whatever him and Billy decide."

Ricky looks in peak shape as he warms his hands on a bag wearing just shorts and boxing boots. After ten weeks of training there doesn't appear to be a scrap of fat on him. Kerry has him where he wants him.

"You hear some fantastic exaggerations about body fat: three percent, five percent. It's absolute nonsense. It's a guesstimate.

"When you look at a bodybuilder on stage, and you've seen how low their body fat is, if he's got to five or six percent, that's a good achievement. So in reality Ricky will be about ten, eleven or twelve percent body fat.

"All these exaggerations about body fat – it's not healthy.

"We have to get his body down to a level where

his body still has reserves of energy. While it's nice to see him looking good, you've got to remember boxing's a physical sport not a visual sport.

"He's still got another three or four pounds to get off to make the weight and then we'll get him back up.

"We monitor him every day and to be truthful we can do it visually. A couple of times – and Ricky will tell you – he's come in the gym and I've said, 'you liar, you've had another meal haven't you?'

"Ricky will come in and train and sometimes I'll say, 'I think you're light'. He'll step on the scales and he is light.

"Being big-headed, I've pretty much got an eye for it. I'll tell him if he's light, to have a meal or to slow down, speed up.

"Although next week his workload will come down, so you'd think that maybe his fat loss or rate of losing weight will slow down, it's the opposite.

"The week of a fight, or the week of a bodybuilding competiton, or the week of the FA Cup final, your metabolism speeds up. All that nervous energy you burn. So as the training comes down, the nervous energy kicks in so the weight will come off quite easily.

"I would never ever – and I would never be allowed to by Billy Graham – do it dangerously or unhealthily. But we will drop a little bit of water. We'll drop a little bit of fluid from a very hydrated body."

It still hasn't been decided exactly how heavy Ricky should be when he gets in the ring with Collazo on the night of the fight. Presuming he makes the 147 pound limit at the weigh-in the day before the fight, he will then put on around nine pounds over the next 24 hours.

There's a fine line to tread, as Kerry explains, "Boxing is physical and mental. He'll have all the drink meals, the Pro-Recover, the Pro-Fuels. Then towards the end of the evening, if he wants some junk food, pizzas and things like that, technically he'd be better off not doing that, but what price his mental attitude?

"So he'll have a little bit of junk food towards the end of the night when his body's going to bed and he's got eight hours to digest it so it doesn't cock his digestive system up.

"We're having a little bit of debate at the moment. It's looking like he's gonna get in the ring at about eleven stone two pounds which is what he got in the ring for Kostya Tszyu and Maussa.

"I totally agree with Billy and Ricky – if it aint broke, don't fix it. But he got in the ring at eleven-two from a platform, the day before, at ten stone. He's gonna put fifteen or sixteen pound on from light-welter to the Kostya Tszyu/Maussa fights. This time he'll be ten-seven so something's got to be taken out of the equation 'cos we don't want him to put sixteen pound on and get in the ring at eleven-nine.

"Something's gotta give. Obviously I don't want the nutrients to be left out, so I've told him if something's gotta give it's gonna have to be his fried breakfast. He's had a fried breakfast on the morning of every single fight he's ever had.

"If he's always put sixteen pound on with a set diet of nutrition and a bit of comfort eating, the good nutrition shouldn't give in my opinion."

But Ricky's stepped up a division and he's fighting a bigger man. Why not put on 16 pounds?

"If we knew for a fact that he was going to take this kid (Collazo) out in three, four or five rounds, then he can get in the ring at twelve stone! But in reality you've always got to cater that it might go twelve rounds.

"Carrying that amount of weight around for twelve rounds could be too much for him. We've got to make sure that he can fight for twelve rounds.

"And we're of the belief that the kid won't be that heavy. The reason we're at the belief that he won't come in that heavy is because when he won the title at ten-stone seven, he'd only got two weeks notice for the fight. So logic tells you that he walks around close to the weight.

"In reality though, even if Collazo gets in the ring at twelve stone, what he won't be is as strong as Ricky. We've seen the sparring Ricky's been doing with the Iranian champion. He's a lot bigger than Ricky, but he could not believe Ricky's strength. Know what I mean?

"I'm very very happy. The brief was to drop his body fat while increasing the muscle. The muscle's there for all to see, and his explosiveness on the bag. I'm really pleased.

"Even though he's an athlete who gets out of shape, he has what we call muscle memory. It's a lot easier to get someone in shape that's been in shape before.

"I've been asked throughout this campaign, for want of a better word, what I think of Ricky fighting at welterweight. I've said from the beginning that I think Ricky is gonna enjoy fighting at welter.

"Because of his style of fighting – his explosiveness, grappling, aggressive type of fighting – I honestly think it will suit him the stronger he is.

"I don't know much about boxing, I just deliver what Ricky and Billy ask of me. But a strong, squat physique, in any sport, will enjoy being stronger in his performance."

Ricky often jokes about his fluctuating weight. He laughs at the prospect of getting very fat when he retires from boxing. The fact is, he does pile on the pounds very easily, but Kerry doesn't see a problem.

"In reality I believe Ricky is the type of guy that has to get out of shape to get into shape. When he starts his next campaign for a fight, he's that sick of indulging, he wants to get back in the gym.

"I can't imagine him going on a downward spiral when he finishes training. After three months, six months, one year, two years, he'd get sick of it.

"He's a competitive animal and competitive animals don't just stop being competitive because they've given up one sport."

Thursday, 4 May......

10.15pm......

In a bid to ensure the WBA sanction his welterweight fight with Collazo, Ricky's given up his WBA light-welterweight belt.

"My team are reassuring me it will be for a title and it will all be sorted out. As I understand it, the WBA are waiting to make a decision regarding Souleymane M'baye, who's the number one contender [light-middleweight].

"The judge hasn't made his decision yet but we're just waiting to hear. My understanding is that if I'm no longer in M'baye's weight division, how can I fight him?

"We're just waiting for the judge to confirm all that and my advisors and team are dead certain that it's gonna happen. It'll be nice to get it confirmed but it's not a weight on my mind too much.

"At the end of the day, the fight will still go ahead and I still will have beaten the world welterweight champion if I win."

Technically, Ricky is now without a world title for the first time since beating Tony Pepp for the WBU belt in 2001.

Developments don't affect Ricky's mood or application as he goes about his gym routine as normal.

2.45pm......

One more day of hard training to go. Next week it'll be a case of simply ticking over in Boston.

"Training couldn't have gone better," he says.

"I've had exceptional sparring partners. I've felt really good in my sparring.

"The first couple of sessions of sparring, after not fighting a southpaw for a couple of years, were a little bit tricky but come near the end I was like a duck to water. I felt really good.

"I'm strong, my weight's perfect, I've only got six pound to go already. Couldn't have gone any better.

"In the last week me and Billy will do a little bit of pad work, but we'll be talking mainly about the moves and stuff that might work against him [Collazo]. Talking about the kind of stuff he might try and do to counteract my stuff.

"We'll be talking game plans and tactics and I'll do a little bit of road work. We'll just do enough to get my weight down that last few pounds for the weigh-in on Friday.

"Once I've done the 15 rounds on the bodybelt I know I can't possibly be any fitter."

Despite the lingering legal action taken by Frank Warren, Ricky says he's remained focused for this training camp. It wasn't so easy for his last fight.

"Well obviously the problems outside the ring have been a little bit less this time. For the Maussa fight it was nothing short of disastrous the stuff that was going on.

"Although it's still there [legal action], it's sort of died a death to a degree, so I've been a lot more relaxed from that point of view.

"I got a little bit too fired up before the Maussa fight. He [Warren] was seeking an injunction to try and stop the fight. Likewise, there was this wrangling about the alleged contract. This was all about the time it was coming to head.

"Everyday I was picking up the paper and reading certain things that I didn't believe to be true. So it was frustrating.

"It did get to me a little bit and that showed in my first few rounds when I was a little bit over-eager and I got cut.

"It's hard. It's always in the back of your mind. Even for the Maussa fight I was getting a little bit worked up. I was picking up the paper and training had gone well in the gym and my mind was on the fight, but for obvious reasons I wanted to blast out more than Carlos Maussa that night.

"Nothing in life ever runs smooth I suppose so you've just gotta get on with it and deal with it."

On a happier, simpler note, physio on his Spanish Archer - or El Bow - has gone well and isn't a concern anymore.

"Generally in a training camp you have a little niggling injury or something like that, but I've

There's no let up for Billy as Ricky chases him around the ring, pounding the belt ferociously.

nothing really to complain about.

"With a three-month training camp, you know the workload that goes into it, so from an injury point of view and everything, it's been absolutely fantastic."

Friday, 5 May......

News reaches the camp that a judge in the States has given the go ahead for the WBA to sanction next week's Hatton v Collazo contest. Ricky will be fighting for another belt.

1.10pm......

In Denton, there's another belt he's more concerned with today. The body-belt. Fifteen rounds which spells the end of the training-camp proper. The final session on the belt with Billy has taken on a kind of mythical status. This is the day the TV crews, radio and written press turn up for a look at the Hitman.

Along with the media, the punters have spilled in for one last time before Ricky leaves for Boston. The place is as full as a bandit's rifle.

Sitting near one of the ring corners is James Bowes who's here with his grandmother Joyce. He's had some devastating news. Because of his condition, his doctor has advised him not to travel to Boston.

At the far end of the gym is Mike Summerbee, buzzing around the room chatting away to Hatton and City fans. Irish welterweight Henry Coyle has also dropped in to say hello. He bumped into Team Hatton on a recent trip to Las Vegas, and is now training at Ricky's mate Anthony Farnell's gym down the road in Newton Heath.

The room is extra hot and humid as the spectacle begins. Ricky climbs through the ropes and shouts to Paul Speak: "slap a bit of Oasis on – track ten". The track just happens to be *A Bell Will Ring*.

As Liam whines, there's no let up for Billy as Ricky chases him around the ring, pounding the belt ferociously. This is 15, three minute rounds. Of course Ricky will only fight 12 rounds if it goes the distance against Collazo, but training is always geared to 'having three in the bag'.

The end of each round is greeted with a round of applause from the assembled.

With each round, Ricky steps up his work. Oddly, he seems to gain energy with the completion of each round, building up his work rate to a 15th round frenzy. When the buzzer sounds for the end of the session, the punters show their appreciation as Ricky prowls around the ring, working the crowd. He's all fired-up now. He roars at one of his mates in the gym and adopts a menacing scowl. For a split second he looks like a milky-white Tyson.

Billy, meanwhile, is knackered.

The public begin to make their way from the gym as Ricky freshens up before facing the TV cameras.

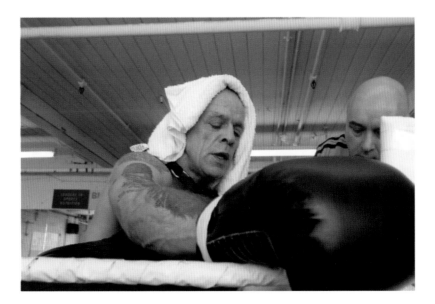

The American Dream

Saturday, 6 May......

One week to fight-night......

10am......

Team Hatton leaves for Boston. Included in the party is Matthew Macklin who'll continue his training in Boston rather than stay home alone.

1.00pm......
(East Coast time, 5 hours behind UK)

The group checks into the Hyatt Regency Hotel in downtown Boston. Once the bags are dropped there's a quick turn around as they've been invited to Suffolk Downs race track – the course where the horse 'Seabiscuit' was discovered.

5pm......

It's Derby Day and the tenth and final six-furlong race is the 'Ricky Hitman Hatton Classic'. Naturally Ricky wants to put a few dollars on and with his football allegiance, he opts for 'Citi Prancer'. Fifty dollars at 6-1. The horse wins.

Ricky presents a prize to the winning jockey Winston Thompson. It's not often the Hitman looks down on a fellow athlete.

The trip couldn't have got off to a better start. "Hope this is a good omen," Ricky says.

9.30pm......

Back at the hotel, Ricky heads for the gym on the 6th floor. He watches *Rocky* while running on a treadmill.

* Jane Couch beats Ukrainian Victoria Oleynik on points in a six-rounder at Birmingham's International Convention Centre.

(Pics. Paul Speak)

Sunday, 7 May......

Midday......

Time for a spot of shopping at Macy's.

He may be a millionaire world boxing champion, but Ricky is no friend of the credit card – he has no plastic. With no dollars either, Speaky has agreed to sort out the purchases on his card.

"Ricky is the shittest shopper in the world," says Paul. "He's a nightmare! He picks up clothes and wanders off. You can't find him again!"

2.30pm......

Team Hatton and a Sky Sports camera crew arrive at Fenway Park, home of the Boston Red Sox. A fine day is had by all but Ricky hasn't a clue about baseball and is more interested in the hot dog and beer sellers who are torturing him by flaunting their fantastic, and very out-of-bounds, products.

9.00pm......

Ricky's being ferried from local radio stations to TV studios as part of his obligation to plug the fight.

Monday, 8 May......

12.30pm......

The Phoenix Camp has made the World's Gym in Somerville, north Boston, its temporary home.

From the outside, the gym looks like a large, single storey industrial unit set in a huge car park. Inside there's a vast gym area full of running, step and rowing machines. A boxing ring's been set up in a room off to the right of the main gym. Inside, the Hatton camp has given it a homely feel with St George and union flags pinned to the walls.

Billy and Ricky do a session on the pads and some bag work.

After training, Ricky heads out to Bunker Hill, site of the first major battle of the American Revolution in 1775. The British inflicted defeat on the colonial forces. Maybe another good omen for Ricky.

It's then back to the hotel for a relaxing evening. Ricky's been keeping himself entertained watching a DVD of the comedy *Early Doors*. You can take the boy out of Manchester......

Tuesday, 9 May......

9.00am......

Glorious Boston spring sunshine has been replaced by dark grey clouds and heavy rain. Home from home. This good omen stuff is getting ridiculous.

12.20pm......

Both Ricky and Luis Collazo are using the same gym to fine-tune their fight preparations. They stagger their sessions: Ricky using the gym first each day.

The British and American press are here in force today to get the pre-fight thoughts of both boxers. Ricky's brought his CDs with him, and works out to......Oasis. He is a creature of habit.

2.10pm.......

Today is Billy Graham's 51st birthday and to mark the event the Sky crew have bought him a cake. They hand the cake to Ricky so he can present it to his trainer, which he does saying, "I'd like to wish Billy a happy 65th birthday!"

Billy looks quite coy as Matthew Hatton and Matthew Macklin laugh and applaud.

The cake is then passed over the ropes to Kevin Francis of the Daily Star so he can put it to one side. Ricky senses an opportunity for mischief and as Kevin takes hold of the cake, Ricky custard pies him. There's chocolate and cream all over Kevin's glasses, face, hair and t-shirt. He looks a mess, but he smells tremendous.

3.00pm......

Now showered and changed, Ricky's sitting in the lobby of the gym with members of the British boxing press - Pat Sheehan *(Sun)*, Ron Lewis *(Times)*, David Anderson *(Mirror)* and food critic Kevin Francis *(Star)*.

"These are the days I've always dreamed of," Ricky says before taking a sip from his Pro-Recover shake. "I'm enjoying it and taking it all in.

"When I first started boxing, if someone had said to me I'd one day be topping the bill in the United States.......it makes you feel over the moon.

"Walking down the street people shout, 'hey Ricky!' In England you half expect it. I certainly didn't expect it in the United States.

"People recognised me at a baseball match. I went to watch the Red Sox. They announced my name over the tannoy to publicise the fight.

"I wouldn't say baseball's my cup o' tea, I wasn't quite sure what was going on, but I can always say I've been to see the Red Sox."

Has the welcome you've received surprised you?

"Yeah. Boston's quite a big boxing city, not along the lines of New York, Las Vegas and that, but you can see it's got a lot of boxing tradition. I get the impression that as a city, they're really looking forward to the fight."

Collazo thinks you're treating him like a joke, and you're looking past him.

"That's what you like to hear from your opponent. He's been saying I can only fight one way and that I'm looking past him. But the fact that I want to fight the likes of Gatti and Mayweather maybe means I've got more ambition than him. Shouldn't he be wanting to fight those guys?

"I'm not looking past him, but those are the fights I want to get to and he's standing in the way. That's not a safe place to be - believe me! It just makes me more determined to get him out of the way.

"No-one's gonna stand in my way. I've worked so hard to get here.

"He's tricky, and I respect him. He'll be a bit difficult to look good against, but what I've seen on the videos, Ricky Hatton at his best and Luis Collazo at his best – he doesn't beat me."

On the subject of Floyd Mayweather Junior, Ricky regales us with the story of when the pair met, ringside, at the Bernard Hopkins v Jermain Taylor

fight at the Mandalay Bay, Las Vegas, in December last year.

"I put my hand out to shake his hand and he never shook it. He just pointed at me and pointed at his chest and said, 'I'm gonna get you!'

"I was like, well that's up to you. I'm just giving you my hand you know, nice to meet you. He said, 'I'll shake your hand after I beat you.'

"So I just said, 'Oh f*** off dickhead!'

"Then, the row I was sat on, I put my legs up. He said, 'I wanna get past'. So I said, 'well walk round then!' A few people from HBO then come over, but it never kicked off. I just told him to f*** off.

"He wants to fight me, I want to fight him and I'm sure it'll happen. It'll be a good fight. I only wanted to shake his hand out of respect.

"Sometimes fighters do that to build up a fight for publicity, stuff like that, but there were no cameras there, no-one watching, there was just me and a couple of his pals. I just thought to myself, 'you're not doing it for the cameras, you really are a dickhead'.

"It surprised me. Even my old friend Junior Witter – I passed him my hand and he even shook it!

"But I'm not bovvered. Don't give a shit."

3.30pm......

The Collazo entourage has now taken over the gym recently vacated by Team Hatton. Oasis is replaced on the sound system by Kanye West.

Luis Collazo is sitting on a stool having his hands bandaged ahead of his training session. He's surrounded by the British reporters.

The New Yorker's wearing a black t-shirt, his tattooed arms and neck on show as he speaks softly.

"Mentally I'm top notch. I always train hard, the only thing different for this fight is that I want it more.

"Whatever it is I have to do in that ring on Saturday night to win – I'll do it."

Collazo doesn't have too much time to chat, but is polite and has a serene confidence. He reveals that he'll celebrate victory over Ricky by treating himself to a new tattoo.

He's asked if he still has space on his body: "I believe so," he replies with a gentle nod and a smile.

"I don't know what I'll get yet, but that's my addiction. I gotta lotta tattoos. The first one I got was the pitbull on my back when I was 17.

"Maybe I'll get a 'ruin the tea party' tattoo. Don King keeps bringing it up so I wanna ruin the tea party for Ricky."

Wednesday, 10 May......

9.00am......

The cold rain falls incessantly from bleak skies overhead.

Midday......

Ricky ticks over with a light session in the World's Gym.

4.00pm......

Ricky's presented with his 'Fighter of the Year' award plaque from the Boxing Writers Association of America

6.00pm......

Back in the hotel, Ricky's sitting in the lobby with his family. The group has grown as friends have started to arrive ahead of the weekend. The four long sofas positioned in a square have become the unofficial Team Hatton Boston HQ. The weather's keeping everyone indoors, but the mood is good.

For Ricky, the biggest problem he now faces is boredom from waiting. He basically cannot wait for the fight. "I'm jumping out of my skin."

Ricky's heard about Collazo's brief chat with the British press earlier. He knows his opponent is very confident. He also knows that the American appears to be a humble and gentle man – as far removed from the trash-talking type as Ricky considers himself to be.

Not that will make any difference come Saturday night.

"It doesn't matter to me if he's the nicest guy in the world or the biggest arsehole in the world. It doesn't matter to me. I'm as determined and as nasty as I'll ever be," he says with a cold stare.

"People have said I'm a nice kid when they've met me, polite and everything, but when that bell goes, and this sounds a bit crude, I want to smash my opponent to bits.

"After the fight has finished, and I have smashed him to bits with a bit of luck, I hope he's in perfect health with no injuries and everything's alright. Then I can shake his hand and buy him a drink.

"I found that with a lot of the fighters I've fought, they've become mates. I'm always getting

messages on the website – 'good luck in your next fight' and all that. I've never fallen out with one single opponent. Once you've had that respect when you've shared the ring with them, you tend to be mates for life.

"Even though you've wanted to destroy them beforehand, once it's over you pray to God that there's no injuries. The worst scenario would be for someone to get injured, with some permanent damage. If that was to ever happen – I'm out of there. I don't think I'd be able to box again.

"You do want to smash him to bits when the bell goes, but after, you go over and ask if he's okay, check with the doctor, then great. You're mates."

Thursday, 11 May......

It's still raining.

The WBA has formally sanctioned the Hatton v Collazo fight on the condition that the winner defends the belt against mandatory challenger Oktay Urkal within 120 days, or surrender the title.

(Pic. Paul Speak)

Midday......

Pre-fight Press Conference......

Local, national and international TV crews, radio and members of the written press are packed into a function room at the TD Banknorth Arena, venue for Saturday's fight.

From the exterior, the building is a huge, featureless, light-brick block on the edge of downtown Boston. Construction work is ongoing around the venue. Inside is a busy rail terminal on the ground floor with the main arena built on top.

12.20pm......

All the fighters and promoters for 'Hitman Invasion' are now seated on a three-tiered top table. Don King isn't here. He's tending to his sick wife so it could be a less entertaining or less time consuming affair depending on your point of view.

Representatives from the Arena, HBO, and Ricky's American promoter Art Pellulo from Banner Promotions, take to the stand to give their own particular spin on what's occurring.

Ricky's sitting to the right of the podium, decked out in his navy Lonsdale training gear with obligatory baseball cap. Collazo's on the left wearing shades and a white Adidas tracksuit.

Eventually Ricky's called to the stand. He says his preparations couldn't have gone better, he's tired of waiting now, "The fight can't come quick enough," he says

He thanks Luis for giving him the opportunity to fight for his belt before adding that he'll be 41-0 at the end of the contest.

Ricky takes his seat as Collazo then takes his turn. He says his training camp has been 'beautiful' and believes it could be the fight of the year on Saturday. He then tells Ricky he has a present for him, he leans down and picks up a six-pack of bottled Guinness Original.

He presents it to Ricky with a handshake and says: "I hear you like this. I don't drink, but after the fight we can have tea together!"

Ricky looks impressed and smiles at his gift. It's a nice touch – as Ricky said before – Collazo has class.

Benny Goodman of Don King Productions then gets his few minutes of the limelight. As he's talking, Paul Speak's mobile goes off - the theme tune from *Rocky* blaring out. Ricky's 'favourite'.

Paul, who's sitting on the first row of the press seats in front of the top table, desperately tries to muffle the ring tone. Ricky hears the phone, stares straight at him, then shakes his head.

Goodman continues talking, "The British are here and I wanna give both these guys a round of applause for being gentleman sportsmen," he says.

"They really, truly respect each other; they respect what the sport is about. They're not eating each other's children, biting each other's legs or hitting each other on the back of the head.

"I really wanna applaud them for stating the good things about the sport. Thank you guys." The media applaud.

1.00pm......

Ricky's on good form now that the press formalities are over: "It's different in America," he says, "they don't fire questions at you, you just get up and tell them how training's gone.

"I think I said the right things so that'll go down well for my first fight in America. All I need now is a performance to match.

"There's no slagging off, he's confident and that's how it should be. We should be confident but we should be respectful. That's what your job as a champion is about.

"It's not just what you do in the ring: it's what you do outside of the ring as well."

Ricky's moved to the side of the room where he's been jealously eyeing the vast array of huge pastrami and ham sandwiches laid out on a long buffet table.

He's counting down the days, hours and minutes until the waiting is over.

"I'm sort of enjoying it [Boston]. Well to a degree I'm enjoying it. But there's nothing more to do now, know what I mean? I'm just hanging around for the weigh-in and the fight."

Why aren't you wearing sunglasses indoors like Luis?

"Well that's Americans for you! It's just a different country and they do things differently. Let's just hope he's wearing them after the fight!"

Job done, Ricky heads off to the gym for a light session with Billy and the two Matthews.

1.20pm......

Collazo's still here. He's been deep in conversation with two elderly men who seem in awe of the young fighter. They part after giving Luis a big hug. Like Ricky, he seems to have time for people.

Unlike Ricky, he's been locked away from family and friends during his fight preparations. He's lived the solitary existence in the Pocono Mountains of Philadelphia – Lennox Lewis's old training base.

"Training camp went beautiful," he says, repeating the line he uttered during the press conference. "The last week, like Ricky said before, is going so slow. I'm just being patient and waiting for the day to come.

"I'm not a trash-talker, I do my talking in the ring and that's basically how every fighter should be. I don't know why some fighters wanna fight outside the ring at press conferences 'cos it's not called for.

"Ricky's a class act as well and I just can't wait to get it on, on Saturday night."

A good looking dude, Collazo's quick to flash his Hollywood smile as he speaks. His softly spoken New York accent barely audible at times.

He appears very laid back as he shakes the hand of another well-wisher.

"Yeah. I'm very spiritual, I'm always relaxed and calm and ready to go. I'm 110% ready so I have no worries.

"God gives me a lotta strength. He gives me guidance and He's the one that keeps us breathing. I'm real spiritual and I'm doin' this for Him. He gave me an opportunity to do it, so I'm doin' it. I'm just glad for that.

"I'm just gonna stay to my game plan. It's gonna be a mental game at the end of the day. It's gonna be a great fight, I just gotta stick to my game plan and I should come out with the victory."

How does he feel about his old friend and sparring partner Frankie Figueroa working for Ricky for this fight?

"He [Frankie] is humble but sometimes he gets over his head. He's a cool guy and I take my hat off to him for tryin' to help Ricky for the fight. I believe me and El Gato have got different styles, he's a smaller man and, you know, I hope he helped Ricky get ready for this fight."

Will this fight go the distance?

"I always predict a victory but I never predict a knockout. As long as I come home with the victory I'm happy with that. I'm ready to go 12 rounds, whatever the case may be. That's what I trained for, and that's what I'm going for.

"It's gonna be a historical night. There hasn't

been a big fight here for 15 or 20 years and maybe it'll be fight of the year.

"Ricky said we'll have a drink after the fight, but I don't drink so we'll have some tea and hopefully at the end of the night there'll be great sportsmanship and we'll go on with our careers."

1.45pm......

As the TV camera crews begin to de-rig their lights and reel in their various cables a few familiar faces remain in the room. Among them is former world super-middleweight champion Steve Collins.

"I'm here 'cos I'm a Ricky Hatton fan. I'm doing a pre-fight function, he asked me to be a speaker, but I'd have come over anyway."

The Celtic Warrior knows Boston well. He was based here for five years, learning his craft before heading back to Ireland. He beat British legends Chris Eubank and Nigel Benn – and won rematches with them both – to cement his own fighting legacy.

"My wife wasn't into boxing but now she comes to Ricky Hatton fights and loves boxing because he's such an exciting fighter. That was someone who's become a boxing fan because of Ricky Hatton.

"He's that kind of fighter, it's great for the game. I admire him as a man, as a fighter, as a person. To me, he's the real deal. He's the best thing to happen to British boxing for a long, long time.

"He's not appreciated in the UK as much as he should be. He doesn't look for it, but the guy's a superstar."

There are similarities between Ricky's style and that of Collins. Both aggressive, value for money fighters. Fans' fighters.

"I had the same plan when I was fighting although I think he makes a better job of it than me!

"He's an aggressive fighter and young fighters should watch him because he does everything right.

"Don't kid yourself; you don't get to the level of Ricky Hatton by just being a brawler. Ricky can do whatever it takes to win a fight. He's a brawler because it's more impressive and he's comfortable being a brawler. But if he wants to box, he can do it. He's the complete package.

"The mistake he could make is thinking about him [Collazo] being a southpaw. He should just get out there and do what he does best, make a fight of it and take away the southpaw advantage.

"The more of a tear-up he makes it, the better for Ricky Hatton. If I was Ricky Hatton, I'd get out there

and push him back, stand on his toes and brawl."

Boston hasn't staged a fight of this magnitude since Marvellous Marvin Hagler fought here two decades ago. Steve hasn't seen such a buzz about the place before, but he isn't surprised.

"Hatton can spark interest in any part of the world. Anywhere with any interest in sport and in boxing will love Ricky Hatton 'cos he's the complete package, the real deal and the best thing that's happened to British boxing for a long time.

"He's the best British boxer and he's not appreciated enough."

A final question then Steve – you've just watched the pre-fight press conference, you're excited about the fight, do you ever wish you were still fighting?

"Oh yeah. After the weekend, on Monday morning, I'm making a comeback! It ends by Wednesday!"

He's off now, looking for that six-pack of Guinness he believes is rightfully his.

"I'll have the Guinness!" He says grinning. "I didn't know they sold bottled Guinness over here!"

"My wife wasn't into boxing but now she comes to Ricky Hatton fights and loves boxing because he's such an exciting fighter."
Steve Collins

Hatton HQ – the lobby of the Hyatt Regency Hotel, downtown Boston, MA.

4.00pm......

Hyatt Regency Hotel... ...Hatton HQ

A boxing bill featuring Ricky Hatton always attracts a showbiz crowd. Premiership footballers mingle in the ringside seats with other sporting stars, actors, musicians and all manner of other 'celebrities'.

Travelling to a venue in England is quite different though to taking time out of a busy schedule to fly to the States. Steve Arnold, who plays squeaky butcher Ashley Peacock in Coronation Street, has done just that. And he's loving every minute of it.

"I love watching boxing and I follow Ricky everywhere," he says in a normal-pitched, strong Warrington accent. "I think he's the most exciting fighter we've ever had, plus he's a really top lad, really down to earth.

"He's a crackin' fella and a good mate. He's been brilliant to me with tickets and stuff. He's been great.

"I'm really excited about today – there's just something about it, it makes my hairs stand up."

Steve enjoyed the earlier theatre of the press conference and was particularly impressed with the Guinness offering.

"I was really made up with Collazo then, he seems like a good guy. It was a nice touch with the Guinness.

"Ricky's always the same and I think it rubs off on other fighters cos Ricky's that nice."

The pair have been friends since Steve watched Ricky knockout Ambioris Figuera at the Spectrum Arena in Warrington in 2000.

"I got talking to some of his mates and they said, 'come out and have a drink with us'. So we met up one Saturday night and we've been friends ever since.

"You have a lot of cocky fighters who mouth off and stuff, but he's just a really nice guy. No-one's got a bad word against him and he's not got a bad word against anybody himself.

"The way he fights, he's just awesome in there. Everyone thinks he's a bit of a mauler and all that, but he can really box. He's a really good boxer. I was watching him in the gym yesterday and he was lightening fast and hitting so hard. He's just absolutely fantastic and I think he's gonna rule the world."

A keen amateur boxer, Steve trained at various Warrington clubs from the age of eight until he was 14.

"I never got my nose broken but I had to quit with bad hands 'cos the ref kept standing on them! I wasn't that good.

"The smell of the gym, the craic with the lads, everything about it, I just really enjoyed. Now I buzz off coming to the fights.

"I just started getting more work as an actor so it was basically boxing or acting. I was a better actor than boxer so I chose the old acting.

"My last fight was actually against Michael Brodie. I got beat on points. I can't remember what competition it was in, but he made me see stars for the first time ever. I didn't get put down but he was very good even then Michael."

With no boxing ambitions of his own anymore, Steve's content with beating his meat on the street.

"It's fantastic, I've just signed till October. I've got a load of stuff when I go back. I've got a load of storylines coming up. I've not a clue what they are.

"I've been there eleven and a half years now, which is a long time, but I'm only a baby compared to people like Bill Roach who was in the first episode.

"I absolutely love it. It's like being a member of a big family. But it's a long time to be with people for 12 hours a day so you get really close.

"I've been very fortunate with Ashley 'cos I get the serious stuff and the comedy as well."

If there was a movie about Ricky's life, you'd be ideal....

"I'd love to play him, yeah. It'd be fantastic. I'd have to stay off the sunbed though!"

Fight prediction?

"Ricky! No disrespect to Collazo, but I've got something in my bones that says sixth round.

"You can't not watch him - he's just so exciting. It's forward, forward, forward and he doesn't seem to get hurt or fazed by anything. He's just a great fighter. I think he's the best thing we've ever had, I really do

"After the fight he'll be with his two best mates – Dom Perignon and Guinness. I don't know where we're going on Sunday night but it should be a belter."

The rain keeps falling.

"The smell of the gym, the craic with the lads, everything about it, I just really enjoyed.

Now I buzz off coming to the fights."

Steve Arnold

Steve Arnold and the Celtic Warrior

Friday, 12 May......

9.30am......

The Massachusetts sky darkens, the downpour gets heavier.

Another day of killing time for Ricky, but at least he's been tickled by the news that one of his friends is currently languishing in a local police cell. The gentleman in question was involved in a dispute with a hotel barman over closing times.

Team Hatton's law enforcers have been dispatched to free the Boston One.

2.00pm......

The last of the pre-fight formalities – the weigh-in.

The function room which staged yesterday's press conference at the TD Banknorth Arena has been changed. The top-tables have been shifted to make way for scales which have been placed in the middle of the stage.

The room is packed. Now, for the first time this week, you get the feeling that the fans have really arrived. Around 60 Hatton fans have managed to get past security, many more are locked outside. Manchester voices echo around the room in a buzz of excitement.

Ricky strips down to his shorts, and steps on the scales to a barrage of noise from his supporters as they serenade him with *Blue Moon*. This is exactly what he wants. His fans are here, he feels at home and gives them a big smile as it's announced he's bang on 147 pounds.

Collazo looks serious. No smiling from him today. Like Ricky, he hits the weight exactly. The two fighters' frames are very different. Ricky, not surprisingly with the step-up a division, is more muscular than ever. He looks in supreme shape. His opponent, three inches taller, is wiry and lean and covered in artwork.

At one point, Ricky responds to the 'one Ricky Hatton' chants and, for a bit of fun, sprints across the stage screaming at his mates, "come ooooonnnnnn!!!" The Collazo camp look startled –

"Mentally I'm top notch. I always train hard, the only thing different for this fight is that I want it more. Whatever it is I have to do in that ring on Saturday night to win – I'll do it."

Luis Collazo

at first they think Ricky's coming at them.

Matthew Hatton also makes his own weight limit. His opponent, Jose Medina (a replacement for his original opponent Anthony Bowman) is a couple of pounds over-weight.

2.45pm......

Billy Graham's happy. "I knew he'd make the weight comfortable, it's not been as nerve-wracking as normal. But it's never been a big worry for him making 140 to be honest with ya. So we knew he'd make 147 no problem.

"He [Collazo] is no bigger than Ricky Hatton. Ricky can still do 140 but Collazo isn't gonna have any advantage in size. It doesn't concern me. I think Ricky will be the stronger man in there."

So just how heavy will Ricky be when the bell sounds for the first round?

"I've told Ricky to be whatever his body wants to be," Billy says before adding a trademark, 'know what I mean?'

"He'll obviously be bigger than ever, but we don't want to get to any particular weight. He'll be whatever his body wants him to be.

"I'll have one last chat with him to go over things - mostly to satisfy me to be honest with ya, but I

know he [Ricky] knows everything he has to do with this kid. We're prepared for whatever."

Billy gives the impression that he suffers more from pre-fight nerves than Ricky. He admits that on the day of a bout, he's no social animal.

"I like to stay on my own – know what I mean? I like to be on my own before fights. It's something I've always done. I did it as a fighter."

3.00pm......

Ricky's still on a high after the weigh-in.

"It was just like being in Manchester really. The Brits always come out in force. Whenever Bruno or Lewis or Hamed have been over, they've always had fantastic support so if the weigh-in is anything to go by – with all the singing of *Blue Moon* and 'there's only one Ricky Hatton', to be honest I don't think I've ever had an atmosphere like that weigh-in.

"All the singing and cheerin' of my name got me all psyched up so I ran over to the fans and gave it 'come on!!!! Lets hear yer!!!!'. I ran past Collazo to do it and he must have thought, 'f***in 'ell what a lunatic'. If he thought I was psyched up then, wait until the bell goes."

"I think the style of physique he's got, that extra few pounds will suit him. I think his body language is telling us that."

Kerry Kayes

Saturday, 13 May......

Fight-Night

9.15am......

It's raining. In Boston. Still.

10.20am......

It's not the Butty Box in Hyde, but Boston's luxury Hyatt Regency will have to do. Ricky wants his fry-up.

It's the typical hotel buffet system. Unfortunately, as this is America, there's no black pudding.

10.50am......

As Ricky continues to grease his stomach, Kerry Kayes has had enough and leaves the restaurant. As ever he's chirpy and relaxed. The weigh-in went to plan, Kerry's done his job.

"I'm relieved, obviously, that he made the 147," he says. "About ten or twelve weeks ago I was chatting to a few reporters with Billy and I actually thought that the 147 from a body point of view and mentally, would suit him.

"I think everyone can see that it has and I think he'll prove it in the fight. I think the style of physique he's got, that extra few pounds will suit him. I think his body language is telling us that."

As you would expect from a former national bodybuilding champion, Kerry is a perfectionist. He takes great pride in getting Ricky as strong and perfectly conditioned as possible.

The weigh-in is Kerry's moment. In a way, it's his fight-night.

"It is yeah 'cos I do his nutrition and I do his weight management. It's my job to get him on and off the scales and you could take the safe road and aim for 146, 145 and it'd be dead relaxed.

"But the aim of the game is to get him as close to the weight as you possibly can. We did a lot of work that morning and when he stood on the scales at 147, I just thought I'd hit the bullseye!

"We weighed him on the morning and he was

right where he wanted to be. There was loads of water in him so there was plenty to play with.

"We got the driver to take us to the venue and we got there at about 12 o'clock. He stepped on the scales at 12 o'clock and was two pounds over. That was exactly what we wanted.

"So we came back here [to the hotel] and he went into the sauna for twelve minutes and the water just flew out of him.

"We then went back to the venue for the official weigh-in. When I heard '147' I was relieved. I was happy, yeah.

"That's my personal pride. There's been a little bit more in the media about this fight and his weight management. Is he gonna be a 140 fighter with an extra seven pounds of body fat – you know what I mean? But when I looked at him, he looked like a welterweight and that was my personal pride."

There'd been some debate before the team landed in Boston as to whether Ricky's fry-up would have to go this time. Obviously that's not the case. He's still in the restaurant wolfing down sausages.

"He's had all the good nutrients he requires and a bit of comfort food on top, so we're feeding his body and he's feeding his mind. It's with my blessing. We have a bit of a laugh and a joke about it.

"After the weigh-in, I've pretty much lost control to be truthful," he laughs.

Kerry's job isn't over just yet though. On fight-nights he acts as Billy's assistant, so it's up to him to make sure the team have everything they need for the dressing room and the corner – bandages, tapes, scissors.

"I'll also manipulate Ricky's arm either now or at six o'clock. If I'm not needed for anything else, because if truth be known I'm a bit tired, I'll go out for lunch with my wife and have a bottle of wine which will be a bit of a sedative. Then I'll try and get a couple of hours' sleep this afternoon.

"The undercard has to be at the arena for about five-thirty this evening. Ricky will turn up about nine o'clock.

"I've noticed boxers seem to be more relaxed on the day of a fight than on the day of the weigh-in.

"After the weigh-in they can then have a bit of comfort eating and that gives them a better night's sleep. You could say they shouldn't have it, but from a body point of view, if you get a good night's sleep – what price is that?"

11.25am......

Ricky's finished his breakfast and is taking it easy on a sofa in HQ.

"I had egg, bacon, sausage, hash browns, so it's not too bad. It's not the same [as the Butty Box] 'cos you can't beat an English fry-up, but it's good enough. A bit of grease inside me makes me feel better.

"Last night I had pasta – lasagne with bread and starchy foods and that, so today it was nice to get a bit of shit down me after 12 weeks of dieting."

Some of Ricky's friends are still in the land of nod. While he was climbing into bed for his early night, they were heading out for a lively evening on the town. This time tomorrow though, he'll be with them - every step of the Guinness-sodden way.

Other members of the travelling party have been up early and are already in one of Boston's many Irish bars watching the FA Cup final.

12.55pm......

News filters through that Liverpool have come back from 2-0 down to draw level with West Ham in the Cup final. The match ends 3-3.

After extra-time Liverpool win on penalties. The news doesn't delight anybody present.

Team Hatton solicitor Gareth Williams

1.05pm......

Team Hatton's solicitor arrives back in the lobby after a trip out to the shops. Luckily, Gareth Williams has been wearing his 'Hitman' rain jacket to protect him from the miserable weather.

He's been a busy man over the last few months, dealing with the various legal issues affecting the Hattons.

"The main case in England," Gareth says, "is that Frank Warren (Sports Network Ltd.) has sued Ricky and his dad and Punch Promotions.

"Essentially what he's saying is that he has a three fight deal and he's looking for breach of contract damages.

"Initially he was looking to stop the fight and get an injunction. We've defeated him on that, now he's continuing with a simple breach of contract claim.

"I've chased him to exchange witness statements and I'm pushing to get it resolved as quickly as possible.

"We're probably looking at a trial before October.

"That's the main English claim. It gets more complicated because Frank Warren has now issued proceedings against Ricky's dad Ray alleging libel. That's at its very infant stages but with a similar approach. We've defended it, put in a big defence and heard nothing at this stage.

"It's further complicated because we've heard one or two things Frank Warren's said which we consider to be libellous against him, not that we want to rush out and start suing people, but there comes a time when you have to fight fire with fire.

"If he wants to start suing us for everything then we'll respond in kind. We're confident we can beat him at every stage.

"What he's also done – there's a French guy, same weight as Rick called Souleymane M'baye and he [Frank Warren] signed him up in September.

"M'baye's brought proceedings in New York where he's suing the WBA. He's just amended that claim to start a fresh claim against Rick, Dennis Hobson and Robert Waterman.

"When we landed in New York on Tuesday the phone didn't stop ringing. The American lawyers who I used as my agents last time had just been served with documents a foot thick for a hearing the following day.

10.00pm......

Ricky has put on his gloves and blue, spangly, white-tassled shorts, complete with glittering union flags on each leg. The name of his boy Campbell is stitched into the shorts with 'Hitman' emblazoned across the waistband.

HBO sends a crew into the room to film Ricky staring menacingly down the lens throwing jabs and hooks perilously close to the camera.

With that out the way, he concentrates on hitting the pads with Billy. It's getting close. The mood has changed, the banter's died down, his friends leave the room.

10.25pm......

The Arena looks about half-full, maybe ten thousand spectators at best. The weather has certainly affected walk-up sales on the night, but the atmosphere is still crackling. Union flags and crosses of St George are being unfurled all around the venue as the chant of 'there's only one Ricky Hatton' begins.

10.30pm......

The spiced-up version of *Blue Moon* signals the start of the ring-walk. But it's barely audible above the crowd noise. It's not the MEN Arena, but the three thousand or so Hatton fans who've made the journey are doing their best to make their hero feel at home.

Team Hatton enters the ring. Speaky stands in the middle, holding wide a union flag with a message from Ricky to his fans printed across it. 'your support got me here – thanks', it reads.

Collazo's ring-walk is drowned out by the Hatton crowd and his name is greeted by boos when announced.

Don King's in the ring. With his manic, toothy grin he's waving an American flag in one hand, a Puerto Rican one in the other.

The crowd settles down, the fighters touch gloves in the middle and the bell rings.

10.50pm… Round One… It couldn't have got off to a more dramatic start as Ricky floors Collazo with a left hook after 20 seconds of the fight. The American's quickly back on his feet – he's not been hurt, more caught cold. He recovers to land a couple of solid punches of his own, but Ricky works the body well. It's his round.

Round Two… Collazo's down again, but it's a slip. Ricky moves forward relentlessly. Collazo shows he can take a blow as he shrugs off a big right close to the bell.

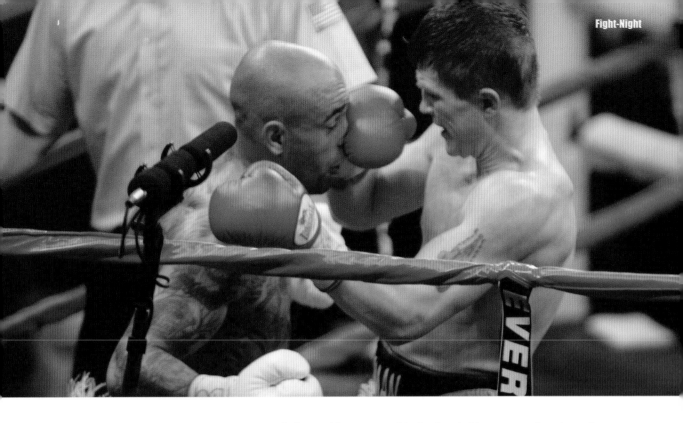

Round Three... A clash of heads leaves Collazo with a cut on his forehead. It's scrappy, the champion counters with some neat shots showing impressive handspeed. The crowd continues to roar for Ricky. The New Yorker doesn't seem to have any fans here in Boston.

Round Four... A round of clinches and spoiling until Collazo catches Ricky with a strong right hook.

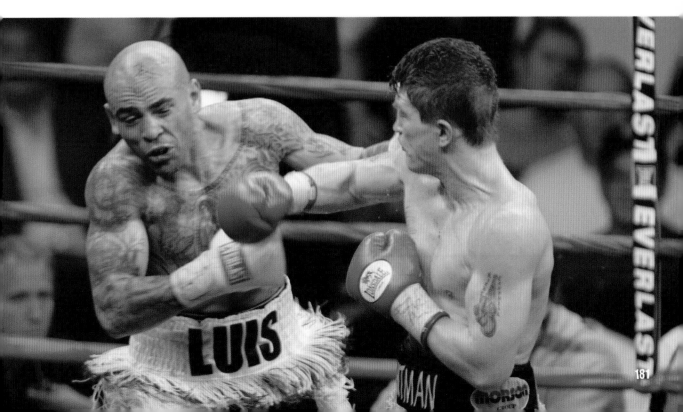

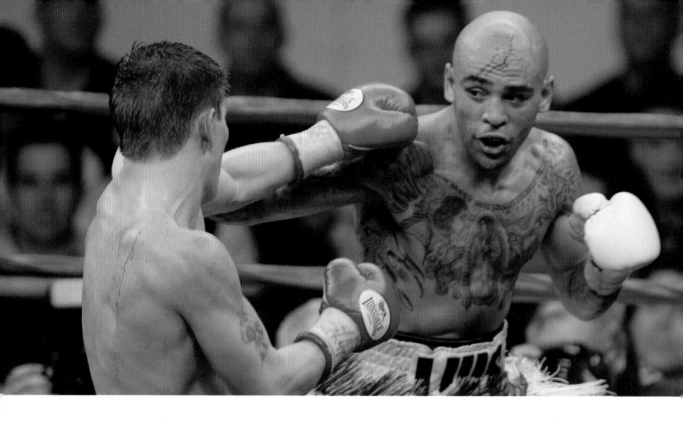

Round Five... The blood's wiped from Collazo's cut head, but he's on top, connecting with the cleaner punches and quick combinations.

Round Six... Ricky's not taking a step back despite the power in his opponent's clever jabs and hooks. He breaches Collazo's defence towards the end of the round and gives his ribs a tickle.

Round Seven... Still Ricky tries to pile on the pressure but Collazo is versatile. He can go toe-to-toe or work well on the back-foot. There's concern on the faces of the Hatton family at ringside.

Round Eight... Ricky's still throwing more punches but he's feeling the power of the bigger man when Collazo lands with accurate shots.

Round Nine... It's still 100 mile-an-hour stuff as Hatton continues to press forward. Collazo's still getting through, connecting with good shots.

Round Ten... There's a bit of a wrestle and Collazo ends up on the canvas, but it isn't a knockdown. Ricky's not finding his target enough, Collazo's working well on the counter.

Round Eleven... The pace continues with Ricky proving again that he throws more punches than any of his contemporaries. He could do with a couple landing just a little more cleanly.

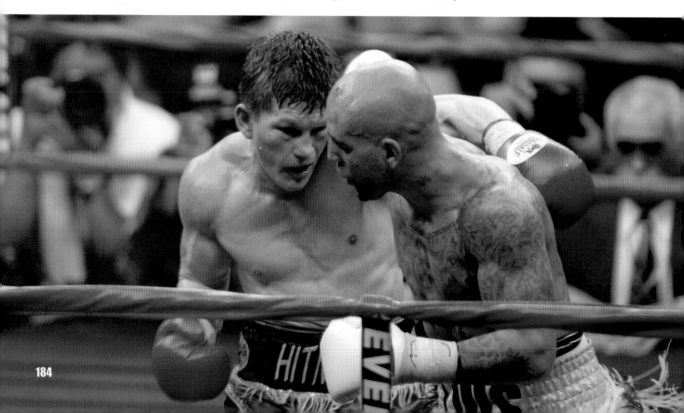

Round Twelve... A nightmare round for Ricky who's bundled to the floor – but avoids a knockdown - during a whirlwind of punches from Collazo. As the round progresses, Hatton fans have their heads in their hands as Ricky's rocked by two solid lefts from his opponent. He's got to hold on as Collazo senses blood. It looks like the American might stop him. Collazo's people ringside are jumping all over the place, but Ricky rides out the storm and the bell signals the end of the fight.

What a fight! But who won?

Ricky's girlfriend Jennifer, mum Carol and dad Ray feel the tension as the drama unfolds.

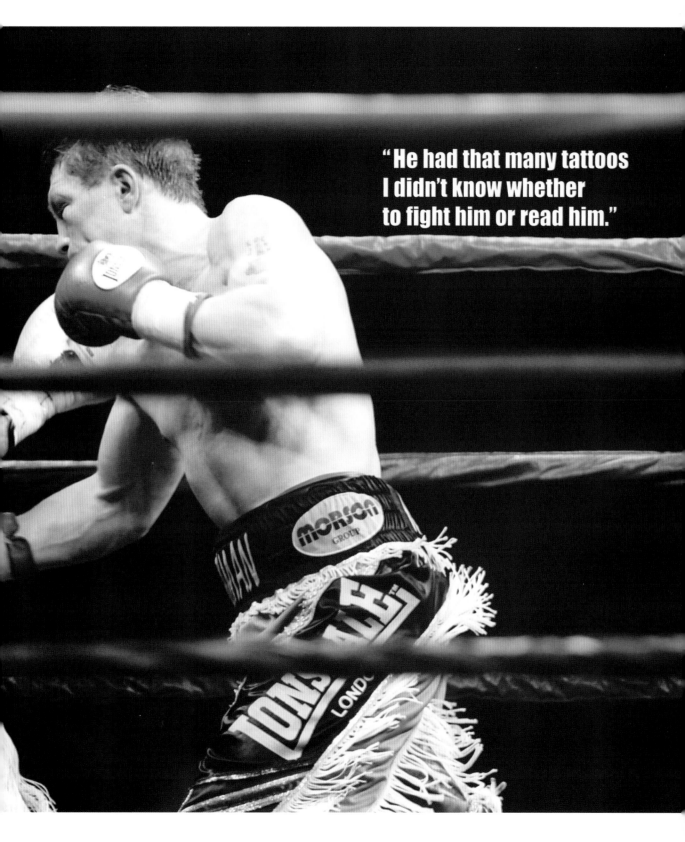

"He had that many tattoos
I didn't know whether
to fight him or read him."

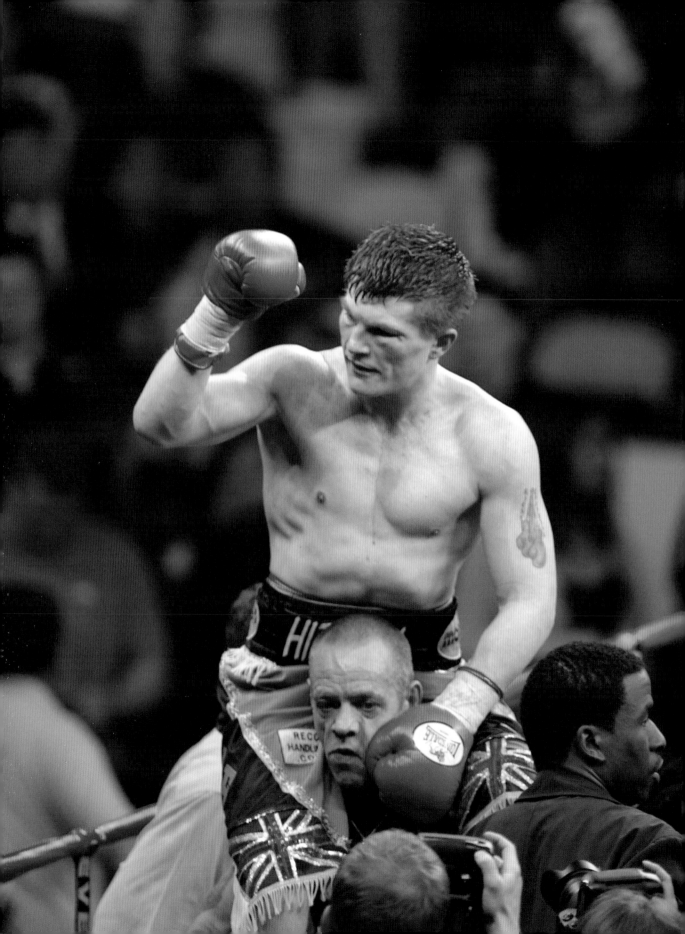

11.40pm......

Ricky climbs on Billy's shoulders and raises tired arms in a victory salute – Collazo does the same as the respective cornermen and promoters dive through the ropes into the ring.

After a couple of minutes, Michael Buffer has the judges' scorecards. The fight is close. A few Ricky fans ringside are convinced they've witnessed his first ever professional defeat. It's too close to call.

The Hatton family are a bag of nerves and the Arena goes quiet as Buffer reads that Don O'Neil scores the contest 115-112, judge Paul Driscoll scores it at 115-112 and Leo Gerstel has the fight as 114-113.

"By a unanimous decision... The winner... and NEW..."

Pandemonium breaks out and no-one can hear the MC finish his sentence. Ray and Carol Hatton embrace. Ricky's girlfriend Jennifer hugs Matthew's girlfriend Gemma, while in the ring, Billy, Kerry, Matthew and Matthew Macklin leap all over Ricky.

After a couple of quick TV interviews, Ricky grabs the MC's microphone and thanks the travelling fans 'who've done me proud'.

"By a unanimous decision......

the winner......

and NEW......"

Sunday, 14 May......

12.10am......

Ricky's been back in his dressing room for 15 minutes. He hasn't moved from his fold-down yellow chair as he continues to press a bag full of ice to his puffed-up, purple eyes.

Only those closest to Ricky are here now, his parents, Matthew, Jennifer and his Team. Among them is Matthew Macklin who checks his watch and realises it's his birthday. He's 24.

Billy Graham's sitting on the opposite side of the room looking at his fighter with a mix of relief and pride.

"I had a better view than anybody else unfortunately," he says with a shake of his weary head. "It was a real tough fight.

"He [Ricky] caught him with a left-hook early and... I can't get it into words... it was probably the worst thing that could've happened.

"The thing we kept saying to him before the fight – weeks ago – was don't get too excited, don't get too over-eager, know what I mean? Well he did get a bit over-eager didn't he?

"I tried my best to calm him down but he wasn't havin' it. He was in his f****** Tasmanian Devil mode.

"I knew right from day one it was gonna be tricky, but he [Collazo] was much more durable than I thought. The kid wanted it real bad. I think the kid learnt and will be a better fighter, down the line, because of it.

"Anyway, Ricky's an entertainer and he certainly entertained the crowd again."

How fearful were you that Ricky wouldn't get the decision?

"I knew he'd got it because Macklin was in the corner with me and he was looking at the score cards. He kept telling me on my deaf side. I had to keep twistin' my head to try and find out!

"It was an incredibly tough last round but Ricky knows what to do when he gets hurt. A lot of people, when they get hurt, run away.. That's the worst thing to do. He gets close and smothers their work.

"You can only fight the way your opponent lets you fight, so taking nothing away from the kid, the kid was a real good fighter. Anyway, we got the title and that's it."

Billy didn't want the fight in the first place. He made that abundantly clear. He's been insisting from the day Collazo was announced that Ricky is a light-welterweight. So what now?

"I know what I want in the future," he says while toying with a plastic lighter, "but I'll keep that to myself for now."

"But over my dead f****** body there'll be a rematch!"

The Preacher rises from his pew and heads off into the shower/toilet area. Ricky's still seated.

"I knew I was ahead and I just had to stay focused," he says looking up now. "Even in that last round, he never shook me. He hurt me, he was quick and he can fight.

"He rose to the challenge, like me with Kostya Tszyu. If I'd kept it simple I could've made it an easy night, but I never f****** do!

"When I boxed a bit I made it easier, but I swear to God he didn't shake me. But when he hit me, I thought - 'oh f***** hell.'"

Ray Hatton, who has been pacing around the room, wears a look of sheer parental relief after a tricky night's work. HBO, he says, are also leaving the old Boston Garden happy.

"At the end of the fight I went over to Kerry Davies [HBO] and said, 'that alright for you?' He looked at me and said, 'oh yeah!' He was quite happy."

Carol Hatton moves away from her boy and it's Billy's turn to take the seat next to the champion. In many ways it looks, from the other side of the room, like a courtier talking to a wounded king as Ricky, hunched, presses an icepack back on that closing left eye.

"Four belts at two weights," Billy growls. "They can't take that away from you!" Billy shakes his head. "But you're a rum ****!"

This cracks Ricky up, he forgets about the bruises and laughs out loud. "F****** inspiring words from me trainer there! You're a rum **** is all he can manage. F*** me!" Billy smiles and says nothing.

"He rose to the challenge, like me with Kostya Tszyu.

If I'd kept it simple I could've made it an easy night, but I never do!"

Speaky is carefully gathering together all Ricky's worn kit from the night. Everything from shorts, robe, boots, socks, gloves and bandages are carefully packed away. Memorabilia is a big business.

The new champion eventually leaves his seat – Billy's wise words not ringing in his head in quite the same fashion as those Collazo punches – and heads for the shower.

The room is now almost completely cleared away and ready for the Boston Bruins or Celtics or whoever.

In the shower, Ricky's still talking through the fight with Kerry who's on hand to make sure he's okay.

After ten minutes or so, he heads back into the main body of the dressing room and sits with a towel around his waist and another resting around his heaving shoulders. He starts to shiver and shake, almost spasm-like, as 12 rounds of ferocious action takes its toll on his exhausted body.

After five minutes or so, he's dried off and back on his feet. He pulls on his dark blue jeans, puts on his black shoes and socks, buttons up a crisp, white shirt and throws on a smart charcoal-coloured jacket. He wants to look the part in the post-fight press conference, which he knows will be lively. He checks with Jennifer if he looks alright. She gives him the answer he wants to hear.

He heads once more into the shower/toilet room to check his hair. While in there he notices a pack of Billy's cigarettes on the sink, takes one out for a laugh, pops it in his mouth and leaves the room with a grin… "ooh it's a stressful business this boxing lark!"

12.50am......

Team Hatton is led by an Arena official down a concrete corridor in the bowels of the building to the post-fight press conference. The room is small, crowded, and full of Collazo's people.

On the top table sits Collazo, wearing dark shades and a black beanie hat pulled down tight, his trainer Nirmal Lorrick is sitting to his left. Don King, Art Pellulo and Dennis Hobson stand behind them.

A sheet of paper is passed around the room revealing the night's fight stats. Collazo threw 712 punches to Hatton's 741. Collazo landed 213 to Hatton's 259.

As Ricky enters the room (no shades) a girl at the back of the room shouts, "we wanna rematch Ricky!" This prompts more heckling.

Ricky approaches the microphone as Don King quietens the crowd, "Let him talk, let him talk!"

Ricky gets straight to it.

RH: I can't wait to see the tape. Apart from being a fighter, I'm a fight fan. If you don't enjoy a fight like that then there's something wrong with you, so credit to Luis for a fantastic fight.

Don's off again, "hear hear" he shouts while applauding heartily.

RH: I don't think anybody gives him as much credit as he deserves....[turning to Luis]....you showed what you were all about, so thank you for the opportunity to fight for your title.

Being a champion, I'll fight absolutely anybody. From day one I've always said I wanted to fight the best and be the best.

That's my third world title fight in consecutive fights and I moved up a weight to do it. I think that shows what I'm all about as a fighter. Whoever they put in front of me, I'll fight, that's what makes your legacy as a champion. Also, what makes your legacy is fights like that. So much respect to Luis.

Thank you to the people of Boston and everybody who's made me so welcome since I've been here, and I look forward to coming over again. Thank you.

The whole room applauds. An American journalist shouts up

Q: Ricky was that the toughest fight of your career?"

RH: Yeah I would say so. The Kostya Tszyu fight was obviously a very, very tough one, but this was a different fight for different reasons. He had a tricky style and it was my first fight at welterweight.

Normally when you move up a division you ease yourself into the action. I've moved up a weight and immediately fought a world champion in Luis, and I think he's showed tonight he's a very underrated fighter.

But that's what I'm all about, I'm always looking for new challenges and I'd say that was the toughest fight of my life.

I fought Kostya Tszyu then I unifed the belts against Maussa. Then my first fight at welterweight is against a world champion like Luis. I don't think I can do much more than that."

"Very good Ricky" shouts Don.

RH: I'll fight anybody and that includes a rematch with Luis".

Cue cheers and applause from the floor. Billy Graham does not look impressed.

Q: Ricky, when you knocked him down in the first round did you think it was gonna be an easy night?

RH: No, but it was probably the worst thing you could do. You go out there, you're just easing yourself into the fight and you score a quick knockdown like that. You get a bit of a rush to the head, steam in there and you lose your way a little bit.
The fight ebbed and flowed, I'll have to watch it on the tape, but basically I think I won it by a couple of rounds.

Q: How badly were you hurt in round twelve?

RH: It wasn't just the 12th round, he hurt me several times during the fight. He hits a lot harder......I still believe I'm a junior-welterweight, but moving up to welterweight I did notice the difference.
He hurt me several times and sometimes the force of the shot would knock me from one side to the next side. The force of the shot was very different but I think the way he hit me and hurt me in the last round and I was able to stay close and smother him, showed that I still had my wits about me. But yeah, he hurt me several times and I'm man enough to admit it.

Q: You really think you won the fight?

RH: I don't think I won every round but I think I won the fight by a couple of rounds. I wasn't worried about the decision but it was close all the way through and very competitive.
Everybody asked me before the fight for my prediction, but I never give a prediction. There's enough pressure on us at this level to perform and I'm not gonna add to that by saying I'll beat him in

this round or that round.

II just wanted to win and it was a big, big night for me. It's the first time I've topped the bill in the United States, I'd moved up a division to fight a welterweight so who's gonna think that's an easy job?

I think Luis said before the fight I was looking past him, but that's not true. There are big names in the welterweight and light-welterweight division so talking about those big fights is your inspiration to win your next fight. I'm sure Luis had the same incentive to beat me so he could then go on to a unification fight. I give Luis a lot of respect and he's proved his worth.

Q: People said you fought a dirty fight.

RH:I don't think it was a dirty fight. A lot of people said Kostya Tszyu was a dirty fight but sometimes it takes a lot of talent to fight up close, throw a lot of body shots and short hooks.

Who says a fight has to be a technical fight? Luis was strong inside and that's why he stood there. He more than held his own. A dirty fight? I don't think so. It's not a tickling contest is it?"

Q: Do you go down to light-welter now?

RH: I felt strong in this weight division, certainly, but as I can make junior-welterweight comfortably, I'm giving people half a chance 'cos they are bigger than me. But that's something that the team are gonna have to look at. While I can still make junior-welterweight, why move up seven pounds and give opponents half a chance?"

Don King hasn't spoken for a few seconds….. "lets get down to the rematch."

"That's down to the team," Ricky says, then adds, "Yeah, why not?" He follows up to more applause.

"I've got to sit down and rest, look at the fight and see where we go. I want challenges. I don't see how people can complain when I beat Kostya Tszyu, unified the belts against Maussa, moved up a weight and fought another world champion in Luis Collazo. What do you want me to do, fight Klitscho next?"

Press conference over. Teams Hatton and Collazo leave the top table, Ricky and Luis share another handshake in the privacy of a corridor as they walk out of the room.

"Yeah, he hurt me several times and I'm man enough to admit it."

"A dirty fight? I don't think so. It's not a tickling contest is it?"

"I beat Kostya Tszyu, unified the belts against Maussa, moved up a weight and fought another world champion in Luis Collazo. What do you want me to do, fight Klitscho next?"

"Ricky is a diamond in the rough and I would love to polish him! He's capturing the minds of the people and I love the little guy. He's a refreshing breeze in the sport of boxing"

Don King

Don King, meanwhile, still has a few words left to say.

"I thought Ricky Hatton fought a great fight. In my opinion this guy's a class act because he is a refreshing breeze in the sport. This kind of honesty is what's appealing to the boxing fans. To be able to answer your questions forthright candidly.

"I think that's applaudable. He's a jewel, a diamond in the rough and I would love to polish him!

"Class and fights – it ain't about whose fight it is. The public come to see a good fight and they saw a good fight. In my opinion, I think Collazo won the fight. He didn't get the decision but that's what controversy means. Make it again.

"What did Ricky say? Fight him again. When? Next. You know whadda mean?"

King, a master of the soundbite, doesn't appear to be slowing down now he's in his mid-70s.

"They all [Team Hatton] scared 'cos they ain't got the confidence that he has. Whether a fight comes off or not, to the public the only thing that matters is what the writers write and what he [Ricky] said, he came off stronger than ever.

"What you've got is a great calibre of fighter. His daddy is great, and he's great. I love Ray. I love 'em both man!

"When he changes, that's when he's gonna lose. He may not lose the fight with the points on the card, but he'll lose the hearts and minds of the public. He's capturing their hearts because he's honest and forthright. A man of the people.

"I love the little guy man! I love the little guy!"

Can the little guy become a huge star in the US?

"If he keeps talking like he is and fighting like he is, he can conquer anywhere! He has the guts, the intestinal fortitude, the mind and the will, and he's willing to take the risk. Without the risk, there's no reward. The greater the risk, the greater the reward.

"That's what Muhammad Ali did. The forthrightness of Muhammad Ali, brash, braggadocio, but then he fulfilled it. He didn't hide from nobody. That's what makes a fighter – you don't get that by fighting stiffs.

"This is the beginning of a young guy going in. He don't have the talent and skill of Muhammad Ali, but he's coming along. He has the will to win and to fight anybody, like Muhammad Ali. I love the kid. I think he's fabulous and he's a refreshing breeze in the sport of boxing.

"With all the bullshit that goes on and everybody looking for stiffs - and really that's how they got him [Collazo]. They didn't get him because they thought it was gonna be a war. But when the guy fought and fought good and this kid says what he said, you can't beat that with an egg beater."

Don's mind is already firmly on the 'next fight'. If Ricky doesn't have a re-match, who would he like to see him fight?

"Well I can't work one for free," he says with a chuckle. "Know whadda mean? Now you wanna put me into slavery again! I can't let you do that!"

The big man with the electric hair laughs manically for a few seconds, before heading for the exit.

1.15am......

Team Hatton leaves the arena – but duty still calls.

"I'd like to thank the people of Boston for all their support and hospitality.

And to all who've travelled over from England, I hope I've done you proud again.

It felt just like being back in Manchester!"

1.30am......

Seaport Hotel, Boston waterfront......

An after-fight party for the travelling Brits is in full swing in a large open function room in the convention centre attached to the hotel. A few hundred have made their way across town to be here.

The room parts when the guest of honour makes his entrance. Cameras flash and huge cheers go up as Ricky makes his way through the room.

The rest of the Hatton clan are already here, sitting at a large table, near the bar at the top of the room. Ricky takes a seat, and immediately his fans are queuing up to congratulate him.

Ricky's eyes are badly marked and closing, but he couldn't care less. His smile's as broad as Boston Bay as he shakes every hand thrust in front of him.

After a quick drink, he's handed a microphone.

"I'd like to thank the people of Boston for all their support and hospitality. I do hope I come back to Boston again."

An American shouts "yes sir" as the fans cheer.

"And to all the people who've travelled over from England, I hope I've done you proud again. Believe you me, I'll still continue to bring belts back for you. It felt just like being back in Manchester!" Again, a huge roar.

"It always means a lot to me. I always get the mic after a bout because the love of the fans is priceless. I've rewarded your loyal support with a belt tonight. Enjoy the rest of the night."

Ricky sits down as the familiar 'there's only one Ricky Hatton' chant goes up.

(Pic. Paul Speak)

1.00pm......

Hyatt Regency Hotel......

The friends and family of Ricky Hatton appear to have left their lobby HQ for a more secluded seating area near one of the hotel bars. Ricky's sitting in the middle. Now he can really enjoy himself.

He's feeling rested and good. He didn't celebrate with a wild party into the small hours, instead heading back from the Seaport to get a decent kip.

The British written press arrive at the hotel for Ricky's post-fight thoughts. He's happy to oblige and heads over to another part of the bar area where he holds court.

"I never make life easy for myself do I? It never rains, it pours. But I feel fantastic, that's my fourth title at two different weights.

"I've got to watch the fight, but I believe it was fantastic. Nobody remembers 12 round bores. Its fights like that, that make your legacy.

"It was as hard as the Kostya Tszyu fight 'cos styles make fights. Fighting a southpaw and counter-puncher, those styles you really need like a hole in the head.

"There was a lot of talk before the fight how he wasn't my first choice of opponent, not because I had fear, but it's just that on your debut in America, the first fight at that weight, you don't want that type of style really. I was put in a position where certain opponents pulled out, I had to vacate my belts and I couldn't fight the mandatories. I was put in a position where I had to fight him. He's a lot better fighter than people give him credit for."

Ricky's eyes are swollen, purple and pink, but the smile's never far from his face as he leans back in his City away shirt and takes a sip of the coffee

Speaky's just handed him.

"I felt I always had my nose in front but he was very good tactically. I started off well then he altered his game plan, then he'd get a stranglehold in the fight and I'd up it a little bit more. When he was having a little bit of success I'd put my foot on the gas and pull away that little bit more. If you noticed, he changed his tactics so many times.

"He caught me, but I can honestly say with my hand on my heart, he shook me but it was more the strength of the shots, the weight of the shots that swung me from side to side. I think the way I handled it by staying close and riding out the storm, I think you could see I had my faculties still. But it wasn't just in the last round; he caught me with several good shots that hurt me throughout the fight. But he never really hurt me. It looked like I was in a whole lotta trouble in the last round, and I was, he was going for broke, but I think it was the weight of the shots that shifted me.

"I felt stronger than him in the clinches. I was hitting him and he was grimacing and grunting but in the back of my mind I'm thinking, 'I can still do ten stone so why am I giving him half a chance?'

"He's a lot better than we give him credit for so obviously he's gonna shout blue murder for a rematch. I'm not ruling that out.

"I don't wanna turn round and say I don't wanna fight southpaws. You fight who you fight. But with my style, you need those styles like a hole in the head."

After another swig of coffee, Ricky turns his head to look out of the window. The rain is lashing down still. He shakes his head.

Then a few feet away, a familiar sound as Paul Speak's mobile phone goes off...

"f****** hell Speaky!"........Ricky turns back to the journalists sitting around him.

"You know when you go to Las Vegas and you hear the slot machines......that's his f****** phone. I've heard it all week!"

What next for the WBA welterweight champion of the world? Does he stay at 147 or head back to light-welterweight?

"At welterweight I'm giving them half a chance," Ricky shrugs. "But I'm not saying I'm going to come back at junior-welterweight. It was the same before the fight as it is now. If the better fighters are at junior-welterweight I'll come down, if they're at welterweight I'll stay there.

"I've showed my champion spirit going into every fight when we're putting up with the shit we're having to put up with. Inside the ring and out

(Pic. Paul Speak)

"I was hitting him and he was grimacing and grunting but in the back of my mind I'm thinking – 'I can still do ten stone so why am I giving him half a chance?'"

of it, the whole picture, there are so many things I've had to deal with. It's made me a stronger fighter full stop.

"If a fight with Castillo or Corrales comes up.....those guys are floating around the pound for pound ratings. Then there's Gatti and Boldimir at welterweight, and obviously Mayweather is the pot of gold at the end of the rainbow.

"Boxing is what it is. People are more interested in fighters than belts but you tell that to someone who's just sweated blood for a belt."

It's Sunday afternoon, after winning a fight. If he was at home, he'd have a 'bad shirt' party at the New Inn in Hattersley.

As it is, he's going to take it easy and have a few drinks with his family and friends in the hotel. Tonight he hits the town with the lads. This is Ricky's day.

Monday, 15 May......

Matthew Hatton celebrates his 25th birthday.

7.45am......

American businessmen and Japanese tourists wait at the elevators on the sixth floor of Boston's Regency Hyatt Hotel. They're heading to breakfast at the start of their day.

To their left, asleep in an armchair, is the 6'1", shaven headed, 17 stone, 49 year old policeman, Paul Speak. Snoring........wearing only a pair of underpants.

It was a lively evening in Beantown and Paul wasn't the only victim.

"My favourite day is always the day after a fight," Ricky says. "Although we didn't have a dodgy shirt day, we did go out in our droves. We found this pub and just terrorised the place really.

"We was all drunk, Dennis Hobson was up singing. Me and Dennis had a little bit of a fight and I threw him over the pool table!

"I was stood on the bar singing *Blue Moon* and a few other songs including my version of *Alouette* (very rude). It was just the usual fun with family and friends. A good day."

4pm......

Before he leaves the USA, Ricky has a chance to read what the local press are writing about his fight with Collazo at the New Garden.

The Boston Globe, while not denying Ricky deserved his 'razor-thin unanimous decision' – argues that his performance was too similar to his nickname .

.....For far too much of his fight with Luis Collazo, he was the hit man.

Hit by lead right hands. Hit by short lefts. Hit on the inside and, more often, hit from the outside.........

The paper goes on to say:

.....He confirmed his well-deserved reputation for toughness with an American audience before a roaring house of 6,280 at the Garden (don't believe the 7,850 promoter Art Pelullo cited).

(Pics. Paul Speak)

"We was all drunk, Dennis Hobson was up singing. Me and Dennis had a little bit of a fight and I threw him over the pool table!

I was stood on the bar singing 'Blue Moon' and a few other songs including my version of 'Alouette'. It was just the usual fun with family and friends. A good day."

The Hitman Returns

Tuesday, 16 May......

Team Hatton arrives back in Manchester. Ricky catches up with the British press reports of the Collazo fight.

Most suggest the experiment at welterweight wasn't a complete success – despite victory.

Ricky's own feeling seems to capture the mood, "I can still make light-welter, so why give people half a chance at welter when there's half a stone extra on every punch?"

Thursday, 18 May......

Two days at home and it's time for a trip to the States. Ricky fulfils a promise to take his son to Florida.

Friday, 26 May......

Back in Blighty.

"Me, my mum, my dad and my girlfriend Jennifer took Campbell away for a nice, relaxing holiday. We went to Disney and Epcot and Universal and all that.

"It was brilliant. Just seeing his little face going through the doors of Disneyworld and him seeing the castle and all that, it was brilliant."

Wednesday, 31 May......

Ricky's due to appear at the Sports Café in Manchester to sign the Nationwide England World Cup bus, before it heads off to the finals in Germany.

The old London red double-decker's been travelling around the country collecting signatures and good luck messages from supporters and celebrities. Ricky is not feeling too good though, and is bed-ridden with a cold. The mountain goes to Mohammed – the bus heads out to chez Hatton and Ricky signs his best wishes.

Thursday, 1 June......

A week after returning from Florida, Ricky heads away for another trip to America.

Matthew Macklin meanwhile, takes on Marcin Piatkowski at the Aston Villa Leisure Centre on the undercard of Young Mutley v Kevin Anderson British and Commonwealth Welterweight title fight.

A boisterous home crowd roars as Matt puts in the performance of his career to dismantle the Pole, stopping him in the fourth of eight scheduled rounds.

Wednesday, 7 June......

Back in Hyde.

"I went to Vegas to watch Castillo v Corrales. I went with Dennis Hobson and a couple of my pals. I took Matthew for his birthday. I said I'd treat him.

"The winner of that fight was my preferred choice for my next opponent but obviously the fight didn't take place. Corrales made the weight but Castillo didn't.

"Corrales is gonna stay at lightweight but Castillo is gonna have to move up so I told Dennis that's the fight I want, that's my preference. He's in negotiations now.

"Cotto's also an option and there's Oktay Urkal who's the mandatory for my WBA belt, so there's still plenty of options.

"The one thing about the light-welterweight and welterweight division is that it's not shy of opponents to face."

The trip to Vegas meant Ricky missed out on supporting Matthew Macklin in Birmingham.

Keeping in touch was also a problem.

"I lost my phone in Vegas so I couldn't phone Macklin to wish him good luck. I did find out how he got on later but it was a little bit of a disaster really."

The mobile is one item never normally far from Ricky's grasp, so he was a relieved man when a 'good Samaritan' found it, and handed it in.

"It was lucky I was in America. If I'd lost it in

England, with all the numbers I've got on it, like Wayne Rooney, I'd have been in trouble!"

Apart from watching the fight that never was, the trip to Vegas was an opportunity for Ricky and Dennis to get down to business.

They had a meeting with promoter Bob Arum to discuss the possibility of fighting Castillo.

Ricky says, "He was very happy to talk to us and said he'd speak to HBO about it, and a venue. He looked really keen. We spoke to the right people."

Meeting people was a bit of a theme of the trip. The Collazo fight has boosted Ricky's popularity in America.

"I got my face about and everybody seemed to recognise me. Crazy when you think I've only had one fight over there, but when I went to the press conference (Corrales v Castillo) I got mobbed and had to go through the fire exit door.

"You expect that in England, to a degree, but not in the United States. It's nice to see how far I've come with just one fight. Give me another two or three fights and who knows what it could do.

"Everyone that came up to me said it [the Collazo fight] was absolutely brilliant. The heart I showed, what a good fight it was and the amount of respect they had for Collazo.

"Everyone took him for granted and he didn't get the respect he deserved before the fight. It will be interesting to see who Collazo fights next 'cos I think he'll be an avoided man now.

"But that fight went down a bundle. It couldn't have gone any better if I'd knocked him out in the first round as daft as it sounds. It was such a tough fight. If I'd knocked him out in the first round it would've been pleasing, and taken a lot less out of me, but no-one remembers one-round knockouts. They remember fights like that. So for my first fight in America, the public couldn't have been more excited."

Friday, 9 June......

The World Cup gets underway in Germany. To celebrate England's participation in the tournament, Ricky's flying two St George flags from the front of his house.

He reckons England have a great chance, particularly if Wayne Rooney proves his fitness, although he's not sure about Sven Goran Eriksson.

After the finals, Steve McClaren takes over as head coach.

"I think it was an obvious decision really. He's been under Sven's wing for some time now so he's had the perfect preparation.

"They tried the Portugal coach [Felipe Scolari] who turned them down. If you think of the running, there'd have been Sam Allardyce, who would have been a worthy choice, Steve McClaren or Alan Curbishley.

"I think Steve McClaren's probably been picked cos he's got more knowledge at international level with him being Sven's right hand man.

"It was the best decision out there. There's a lot of good managers but he's worked closely with Sven and he's got the experience of World Cups."

Ricky's hoping to get out to Germany at some stage. His pal Stuart Pearce is working out there as a pundit for ITV during the tournament. He was another name mentioned for the England post.

"Stuart was never gonna be the England manager. He's only had a season in football management. But bearing in mind how well he's done in such a short space of time he'll probably be an England manager of the future.

"Stuart's sensible enough. He'd probably be the first to admit he needs to find his feet in the Premier league first and then in years to come maybe that will be his goal."

In the summer of 2005, after the Kostya Tszyu fight, Ricky and Stuart met up in Thailand where City were taking part in a pre-season tour. Fun was had by all, with the possible exception of the manager.

"I had a knock on the hotel room door at about eleven o'clock at night," Stuart recalled. "I opened the door and it's Ricky and a pal of his. They came in, emptied my mini bar and pissed off again! Ricky likes to play hard."

Sunday, 18 June......

Ricky's back from a boys' knees-up in Marbella.

"I went over there with my friend Lofty, my uncle and Dermot Craven who's a friend of mine. We tend to go after every fight providing it's not in November or December or something like that.

"There's a good group of lads that go, about 16 of us and we always have a good laugh. Since the fight, I've had three holidays. It'll probably quieten down a bit now and in a few weeks I'll find out who I'm fighting."

(Pic. Paul Speak)

Tuesday, 20 June......

In his first TV appearance since the Collazo fight, Ricky's been invited onto late-night irreverent chat show *World Cuppa* on ITV4.

In the green room he watches England draw 2-2 with Sweden before heading out to the sofa for a chat with the host Christian O'Connell.

Ricky's not overly impressed with England's showing in the tournament so far.

"Tonight was another bad 'un really. Second half we fell apart."

Ricky reveals that Wayne Rooney's been texting him to ask if he can come down to the gym and spar. Hitman and the striker are pals.

"He runs from the dugout like he's gonna chin somebody rather than play football! That's what he's all about and it's what you want to see."

Wednesday, 21 June......

Gee Cross, Hyde......

1.20pm......

Ray Hatton opens the door of the Heartbreak Hotel with a cheery smile. Ricky's half-dressed in the living room, buttoning up a shirt.

As his dad tells him not to forget about a phone call he has to make, Ricky pulls on his navy 'Hitman' training jacket before bending down to tie the laces of his white running shoes.

He's not had the most productive of days. Paul Speak dropped him off at 3am this morning after a long drive back from the TV studios in London.

1.30pm......

This afternoon Ricky's heading into the city centre to speak to the *Manchester Evening News* and local TV station *Channel M*. *The Observer Sport Monthly* has also arranged to conduct a phone interview with him.

En-route he's in fine form. He gives his thoughts on the various team formations available to Sven Goran Eriksson and reveals a little more about those Rooney texts.

"He sent me a text asking me how things were going, so I sent him one back asking about his foot. He said he was confident his foot was going to be right.

"He then sent a text asking if he could come down the gym and spar when he got back from Germany. I said, 'am I gonna have to phone your mum to ask if you're allowed out?'

"I got a message back saying, 'f*** off, I'm gonna come down there and take your belt off you!'

"I wrote back, 'you wouldn't get it round your waist ya fat bastard!'

"Wayne's a top lad. Colleen's sound as well. Proper scousers, up for a laugh!"

4.45pm......

Ricky's sitting in the canteen deep within the confines of the *Manchester Evening News* building. He's sitting with his arms outstretched, palms down as he talks.

He's just finished the final interview on his post-Boston thoughts and now has a few minutes to kill until his girlfriend Jennifer arrives to give him a lift home.

It's been just over five weeks since his gruelling battle with Luis Callazo. He looks back now with fondness on the trip to the East Coast – and the post-fight session.

Wednesday, 28 June......

9.00am......

Another media commitment – this time at BBC Radio Manchester. Ricky's in the studio chatting to presenters Eamonn O'Neal and Dianne Oxberry who are covering the breakfast slot for Terry Christian.

After chatting about the Boston experience and his fight with Collazo, the conversation moves on to reality TV shows.

"I've been asked to do the celebrity ice dancing," Ricky reveals. "Depending on when my fight comes up, I can certainly look at that. Can't say my ice skating's much good though."

"I can dance! I reckon I can put a few moves across the dance floor.

"Then again, who's gonna tell me I'm bobbins at dancing? Everyone keeps saying to me, 'you're brilliant Ricky' but I'm sure they're lying!"

Eamonn invites listeners to email or text in questions for Ricky. The usual queries come in – 'how hard was it moving up a division?' and 'how do you keep your feet on the ground?'

Towards the end of his hour in the studio, Ricky's hit with an unusual anonymous text.

Eamonn reads it out, "Can you be gay and a boxer, or do you have to be rough and tough and not gay? I haven't heard of any gay boxers so are we therefore excluded?"

Ricky pauses for a second, then says, "Well, I must get it across. I'm not gay. I've been beaten around the ring a few times, but I'm certainly not gay!"

10.10am......

Ricky's off to meet Freddie Flintoff who's invited him down to Old Trafford as his special guest for the fourth one day international between England and Sri Lanka.

Flintoff's currently nursing an ankle injury, so it'll be a good chance for the pair to catch up.

"He's a superstar," says Ricky. "We'll have the craic today. Like me, he's not scared of making a fool of himself!"

Friday, 30 June......

The body's still healing.

"I've done a couple of runs but basically I've just been going out and enjoying myself.

"For two weeks after the fight my body was still aching. Whenever you fight, through the training camp and everything, it takes your body a fair bit of time to recover, but even more for a fight like that.

"Words can't describe it. You're sort of like happy, but in the same breath you're struggling to pick up your cup of tea! It really does take so much out of your body.

"The three month training camp's hard enough, then you have a fight like that. Your eyes are closed, well certainly one of my eyes was closed. Your hands are hurting. For a couple of hours after the fight you're peeing blood. You wouldn't wish that on anyone.

"Even two weeks after I was still feeling aches and pains all over my body and my hands were hurting. Billy Graham turned round to me and said he didn't want to see me anywhere near the gym.

"I've had a good few weeks off so, slowly but surely I'll start creeping back into the gym now. Do two or three days, see all the lads and just tick over.

"At the end of the day, this game started off as a hobby for me and now I get paid for doing it. It's made a very good living for me and my son and my future family. Painful as it is, it's all worthwhile.

"People just see the fight on the television and they think – 'oh innit hard that!' But what they don't see is how much pain you go through after. You need help being put in a car. You can't lift your cup of tea.

"Then there's beforehand. The dieting, the sparring. Thankfully I've been able to do this book so people can get an idea of what it's all about."

Last Word

Why **Gordon Ramsay** loves the Hitman

Shortly after midnight on Sunday 5 June 2005, Gordon Ramsay makes his way through the crowded concourse of the MEN arena. He's enroute to the VIP section at ground level ahead of Ricky Hatton's fight with Kostya Tszyu.

The bar areas of the venue are particularly packed. As the foul-mouthed, hot-headed TV chef edges past groups of boozed-up lads, he starts to get recognised.

"Oi Ramsay! What you f****** doin' here ya tosser?" One lad shouts at him with a smile. Gordon just laughs back. He gets this all the time.

Another punter spots him: "You w*****! You bastard! Who the f*** do you think you are big boy?"

"Ramsay you're a t***!" Another adds.

It's all meant in good humour, and it's taken that way.

"They were excited; they'd had a bit to drink. We were all there for Ricky," Gordon says.

"I sat next to Russell Crowe [the Pope's the biggest name-dropper I know!] and he turned around and said, 'My God, I've never known a chef to get so much shit in all my life!' I said – 'Listen, you take it on the chin and deal with it. You don't get precious. F*** it!'

"That's the name of the game. I am what I am and I really enjoy what I do and I think it shows."

Gordon Ramsay's face is everywhere. Apart from being a chef of some renown and filling what seems like the entire nightly schedule for Channel 4, he's a huge boxing fan.

He first became aware of Ricky Hatton when the Hitman fought Robert Alvarez on the undercard of the Naseem Hamed v Kevin Kelley clash at Madison Square Garden in December 1997.

"There was this little pasty milk bottle that no-one was paying any attention to. When the bell went off, it was like, 'Jesus Christ! Look at the power of this guy!'

"It was Ricky's tenacity, you could see it then. I said to Frank [Warren], 'Oh my God, that guy is extraordinary!' So ever since then I've followed him in a big way. The way he dealt with that fight was extraordinary."

Ricky won the four-rounder by a unanimous points decision.

"How intimidating for a guy of that age? Madison Square Garden! Fighting like that yet no-one paying attention to him until the second or third round when he just went mad.

"It just goes to prove when he's in that mood he can focus his level of attention like switching on a light bulb. Incredible!

"I worried that he was small and wouldn't fill out, but every six months the guy gets bigger and better. There is no fighter fitter than him out there on the world circuit.

"When I started watching boxing with my father, the guys were fighting 15 rounds. Ricky could quite easily go 16 rounds."

When he's not shouting at people in kitchens, Ramsay, a former Glasgow Rangers footballer, likes to run double marathons for fun.

He knows a thing or two about fitness.

TV filming commitments prevented him from watching Ricky in Boston, but usually he can be seen ringside at all his fights.

"The smart thing about Ricky Hatton is that he has a life outside boxing. Very few boxers do because they stay in their little bubble and become very precious. They walk around in a way that they believe they are untouchable. Ricky falls back into a very normal way of life.

"The minute that bell's gone, in the twelfth round, the following day he goes back into a normal life. He's one of the very few boxers who can switch off and go into a normal mode. That is down to the

(Pic. Mark Robinson)

security, closeness and affection of his family to keep him normal.

"He's a very understated, talented boxer that loves slipping into the mainstream of normal existence outside the fight-zone."

As viewers have witnessed, Ramsay is a high-profile, driven man who understands the importance of letting off steam. There are many similarities with the Hitman.

And, as a man who's made his fortune through fine dining, he also knows about indulgence.

"What's wrong with indulging? The guy needs to lead a normal life. It's nice because he hasn't become precious. A lot of boxers in his position would be so far up their own arse they'd think they were God's gift. This guy has a normal existence and it's an absolute pleasure. I welcome it and wish more boxers would do it to be honest.

"I have a wife and four kids, the most amazing family. All you want, all you long for, is that level of normality. You don't walk around thinking you're famous. You walk around thinking you're busy, you're excited in what you're doing and you're very, very lucky to enjoy something that you do. Not just as a job, but as a passion. Very few jobs across the world hold that, but Ricky has that.

"Last time I saw someone with this level of focus was Sugar Ray Leonard. Ricky wants to retire at the top and not become a victim of the boxing glove. You've got to admire that level of thought.

"He's in Manchester, he has the most amazing grounding, but he's ambitious and he's climbing the world platform. Now it's the States and he's put one foot on the map out there, on the back of the Collazo win. He's going to get bigger and better.

"The good thing about Ricky, is he's still young for God's sake!"

Hitman Fans

John Robert Acton
Mark Adams
Michael Adams
Mark Aldridge
Ian Allcroft
Stephen Allinson
Shaun Anderson
John Appleyard
Mark Armitage
Robert J Arnold
David Ashfield
Gary Ashton
Terence J Ashworth
John Askew
Ged Atkins

David Baggaley
Denis Bailey
Graham Bailey
Edward Baker
Mark Barber
Dean Barlow
Dave Barnes Nic
Darran Barnett
David Barratt
Noel Barrett
Mark Beale
Steve Beales
Scott Beesley
Graham Bell
Thomas J Bell
Mark Bennett
Billy Benson
Martin Benson

Andrew Bentley
Gary Bettis
Bill Billington
Doug Bishop
Paul Bolton
Wayne Bonworth
Amanda Booth
Myles Booth
James Michael Bowker
Lee Boylan
Andy Bradley
Dave Bradley
Roger Braithwaite
Chris Brannick
Bruce Brasher
Rob Brearley
Gary Bright
Stephen Brindle
Chris Bucknall
Mark Bullock
Gary Burke
Ray Burnside
Fred Burrill
James Burrill
Lily Burrill
Rebecca Burrill
Jeremy Butler
Neil Butler

Steve Cahill
Mark Cain
James P Callan
Stuart Cameron
Jason Canny

Gerard Caraher
Jason Carrodus
Paul Carroll
Lol Carter
Jonathan Carter – Mediprop
Jack Cartwright
Tracey Cearley
Liz Charlesworth-Jones
Kevin Charlton
Samthann Ciccone
Mic Clark
Tina Clews
Richard Cloake
Dean Codd
Jon M Coleman
Michael Collins (Ashton)
Richard Conlon
Andrew Coop
Danny Cooper
Greg Cooper
Peter Cooper
Mark L Cope
Danny Corrie
Mark Cowgill
Celia G Cox
Dominic G Cox
Eric Cox
Gregory J Cox
Richard Crane
Martin Crisp
Andrew Cross
Joan Cross
Bill Cunningham
Diane Curry O.B.E

Keith S Dance

Danny

Joe Davenport

Eddie Davies

John Deakin

Richard Dennett

Graham A Dewar

Roger Dickin

Stephen Dolan

Al Dood (City Legend)

Phil Dooley

Frank S Doran

Danny Doyle

Mark Drury

Andrew Dunne

Matthew Dunne

Edith Eaves

Anthony Ebbrell

Simon Edwards

David Eglin

Michael Ellison

David Mark English

John English

Brian Entwistle

Damian Farnworth

Renny Farrington

Brian Fazey

Ryan Finnigan

Tony Fitton

Andrew Fletcher

Matt Fletcher

Ian Floyd

Andy Foden

Graham Foster

Matthew Foster

Ken Fowles

Daniel France (Dingle)

Joe Friar

Arthur L Fryers

Andrew Furnival

John Galloway

Derek (Decca) Gamblin

Bill Garnett

James Garnett

Jonathan Gatcliffe

Craig Gibson

Thomas Gibson

Geoff Gildart

Clint Glaister

Ciara Glendon

Roy Glover

Pamela Shirley Golder

Rodney Gollings

Elliott Gough

Gordon Ellis Green

Andy J D Gregory

Daniel Grimshaw

Barry Guy

Colin Hadfield

Derek Hadfield

Andy Hall

Kenny Halliwell

Steven Lewis Halsall

Andrew Hampson

Stephen Hand

Bill Hannah

Scott Hannah

Lee Hanson

Arthur Harding

Harry Harrison

Jonny Harrison

Neil Harrison

George T Harvey

Mark Hattle

Sarah Havenhand

Stephen Heathcote

Carl Heaton

Greg Heaton

Eric Henshaw

Ken Heppenstall

Tony Hester

Damian Hewitt

Paul Hewitt

Rick Heyes

Roger Hicks

David Higgins

Tony Hill

Kevin Hilton

Matthew Hilton

Tim Hilton

Stephen Giles Hindle

Paul Hitchin

Mark Anthony Hodgkinson

Paul Holt

Aron Hopwood

John Horrox

Edward Houghton

Alan Howard

Gil Howarth

Jon Howarth

Keith Howarth

Fiona Howat

Richard Howells

Thomas Howells

Andrew Hoyland

Peter James Hudson

Andrew Hughes

Cyril Humphreys

Jo & Jay Hyland

Roger Melvyn Ince

Andy Jackson

Tony Jackson

Shaun Jacobs

Jedd

Steven Jenkins

Daniel Jenkinson

Charlotte Jenkyn

Neil Johnson

Anthony Jones

Darren Jones

Gareth Jones

Michael Jones
– Optimum Sourcing Ltd

Tony Keegan (The Lord Raglan)
Paul Kelly
Vinny Kelly
David Kelsall
Stephen Kennedy
Trevor Frederick Kennedy
Matt Keogh
Paul Keogh
Abid Hussain Khan
Gino King
Paul Kipling
Jamie Kiss
Paul Kiss
Derek Kitteringham
David Knebel
Robert Kuehl

Patrick J Lacey
John Lamb
Mark Landsborough
Gareth Lang
Brian Langridge
Chris Large
Michael Large
Dave Leach
Edward Michael Leavy
Michael Lawrence Leavy
Keiran Lennon
John W Lennon
Ruairi Lennon
Stuart J Lennon
Kevin Leonard
Peter Lerner
Irving M Lewis
Mr Christopher Lewis
Stephen Lewtas
Carl Linaker
Garry Lippett
Bob Lloyd

Justin Lloyd
David Lockie
Alan Longworth
Robert Lord
Eve Lund

Gary Machin
Paul MacSparran
Richard Madden
Paul Kenneth Manning
Christopher Alexander Manson
Gary Marlor
Cameron Henry Keith Marshall
Mark Masters
Alan McColl
Matt McGuiness
Pat McGuinness
Darren McShane
Dale Meadows
Gary Melia
James Mellor
Peter Mellor
Peter Middleton
Alex Miller
Gavin Miller
Roy Miller
Don Mollison
Jay Mollison
David Moore
Tom Moore
David Moore (U.S.A)
Lee Morgan
John Morgan
Evan Morris
Scott Andrew Morton
Darren James Moss
Dean Moss
Stephen Robert Moyse
Colin Mudd
Nathan Mudd
Mike Murphy
Mick Musgrave

Sam Newton
Alan Nichols
Frank Nightingale
Lee Nightingale
Stuart James Nimmo (Jersey C.I)
Mathew James Nixon
Colin Nolan
Ken Norman
Derrick Nundy

Daniel O'Brien
Frank O'Sullivan
Viviane Oberty
Aaron Ormrod
Greg Otto
Paul Owen

Stephen Page
Steven Page
Liam Kazbek Panesh
Matthew Zak Panesh
Michael Pendlebury
Andy Pick
David Pierce
Stuart Pike
George Elliott Pilkington
Will Plumb
Gary Prescott

Kevin Quigley

Ronnie Rawlinson
Mark Rayner
Alex Raynos
Ashley Reece
Stephen Rees
Glyn Reeves
Jim Rigby
Matt Rigby
Paul David Rigby
Nat Roberson
James Robertson

Garry Robinson

Garry Lee Robinson

James Robinson

David "Marple" Rodgers

Andy Rogers

Mike Rourke

Paul Rowan

Steven Rowan

David Roy

Lee Saxton

Sharon Sayed

Victoria Scott

Gary Seaborn

Lee Settle

Christopher Seville (Manchester)

John Sharp

Ady Shaw

Brian Shaw

Ian Michael Shaw

Tony Sheldon

Christopher Lee Shenton

Dan Shier

Andrew Skarratt

Graham Smith

John (Kingo) Smith

John Richard Smith

Lee Smith

Philip Graeme Smith

Ross Andrew Smith

Patrick & Yvonne Smyrl

Pete Smyth

Bernard Sockett

Alan P Spencer

Stephen Spevack

Trev Stabler

Dave Stack

Chris Stainton

Ray Stanley

Dean Stogsdill

Dennis Stone

Paul V A Stott

Chris Stringer

Alan Struckman

Stephen Stylianou

Warren Such

Philip Sugden

First Name Surname

Phil Sutcliffe

Steven Sutcliffe

Stephen Tapper

Andy Taylor

Jeanette Taylor

Lee Taylor

Neil (Choc) Taylor-Edwards

Paul Teece

The Building Maintenance People

Brad Thomas

William David Thompson

Wayne Thornhill

Esme Elizabeth Mia Thwaites

Scott Ticehurst

Adam Tideswell

John Tierney

Kyle Towers

Mark Turkington

Alison Jane Tyrens

Martin Unsworth

Vaxx

Robert Veevers

Graham Wade

Neil Walker

Paul "Leve Lad" Walker

Terry Walker

John Wallis

Alyssa Walsh

Philip R Walsh

Anthony Wardle

Ron Wardle

Andy Wardner

Jonathan Warr

Terence E Warren

Bobby Watkins

Neil Watkins

Wayne Watkins

Adam Watson

Greg Watson

Ian Jack Henry Watts

John Webb

George West

Charlotte Ann Whalley

Stephen Wharton

Tom White

Paul Whitehead

Antoni Wieczorek

Darroll Wike

Darren Wilcock

Sam Wilcox

Michael Wilde

Paul S Wilde

Jon Wilkins

Simon Wilkinson

Andy Williams

Dan Williams

Leo Williams

Bob Willmore

Sam Willoughby

Allison "The Wife" Wilson

David Aloysius Wilson

Nicki Wilson

Thomas Andrew Wilson

Dean Windass

Chris Wood

Luke Wood

Thomas Wood

Brian Worrall

Guy Worsick

Paul Wray

Wugie

Geraint Yates

Nicholas Young

Thanks to Barry Cox of Great Northern Books and
Dom McGuinness for allowing people to get the
chance to have a proper insight into what I go
through during a 12 week training camp.

To all at Team Hatton, which is Billy Graham,
Kerry Kayes, Paul Speak and Gareth Williams.

To Dennis Hobson, Richard Poxon and Art Pellulo;
to Sky, Lonsdale and HBO; and to the lads at the
Phoenix Camp.

To the many fans and friends who made it over to
Boston and, as always, thanks to my family –
Campbell, Matthew, Jen and especially to my
mum and dad, Ray and Carol.

Ricky